Second Helpings

Mike, Ann and Katie,

Thanks for showing us such a fun time. As always, we love spending time with you.

This book seemed appropriate to say "Thanks" since we definitely did our share of "Eating Nebraska"

The Runza Huts are mentioned but our most favorite place to eat, The Dodge's at 5900 The Knolls, has been omitted. It definitely deserves honorary mention here. Everything was wonderful.

Lots of Love

Sharon & Reid

8-9-97

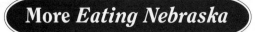

More *Eating Nebraska*

Second Helpings

Wigwam Cafe - Wahoo, Ne.

Richard & Katherine Endacott

• • •

Pleasant Dale Press
Route One, Box 120A
Pleasant Dale, Nebraska   68423

Published in Nebraska, United States of America, by Pleasant Dale Press, Route One Box 120A, Pleasant Dale, Nebraska 68423

Illustrations: Bob Hanna, Lincoln, Nebraska
Cover Design: Brett Dietrich, Lincoln, Nebraska
Copy Editor: Patty Beutler, Lincoln, Nebraska
Production: Record Printing Company, Cairo, Nebraska

01 00 99 98 97 96   6 5 4 3 2 1

ISBN 0-9627861-1-X

Acknowledgements

We gratefully acknowledge all the writers who have provided wonderful work suitable to our subject matter. For being there first our thanks go to Ted Kooser for "A Hairnet with Stars." Bill Kloefkorn retrieved a poem "Breakfast at the Tunnel Inn in Story, Wyoming" which we had heard years ago and remembered fondly. Marge Saiser generously offered several works from her wide repertoire, and we appreciate "In the Cafe" and "The M and L Cafe." Roy Scheele gave permission to reprint his paean to the Cuthills Winery, "Nebraska Wine" which first appeared in *Poetry,* Copyright © 1993 by The Modern Poetry Association. Thanks to Don Welch for his poem "Memo to Marge." It will bring a nod from rural Nebraskans. Thank you to Ron Hansen who gave permission to quote his short story "Nebraska." Art Homer graciously fulfilled our request for a gritty cafe poem and we print "Lunch at Jams Grill, Omaha, Nebraska" with gratitude. We also thank Hilda Raz who gave permission to excerpt a longer poem "Lincoln" which she read at the Mayor's Arts Awards in Lincoln in 1991. We're grateful to three talented essayists who add some spice to our Condiments section: Francis Moul happily coached us on driving Nebraska; Andrew Schultz graciously allowed us to publish his first place submission to the Nebraska Public Radio essay contest; and Richard Conradt gave permission to reprint his article about the MoPac Trail, originally printed in the newsletter of the Great Plains Trails Network.

For detailed check of addresses and phone numbers, we're grateful to Hazel and Louis Brauer. Special thanks to Bob Hanna for his wonderful drawings and patient technical advice. Our applause to Patty Beutler for copy editing, to Brett Dietrich for his design, and to all the folks at Record Printing Company for their attention to detail, especially Margaret Fries.

for

Sarah Denise

"When the talk turns to eating, a subject of the greatest importance, only fools and sick men don't give it the attention it deserves."

—from *Like Water for Chocolate* by Laura Esquivel

"One of the delights of life is eating with friends; second to that is talking about eating. And, for an unsurpassed double whammy, there is talking about eating while you are eating with friends."

—from *Home Cooking: A Writer in the Kitchen* by Laurie Colwin

Table of Contents

Introduction xxiii

NORTHEAST

Nebraska Wine by Roy Scheele...................................... xxvi
Glur's Tavern, Columbus by Robert Hanna 1
Beemer
Marilyn's Tea Room 3
Blair
Cafe on Main.. 4
Catering Catering 4
Columbus
Dusters... 5
Glur's Tavern 6
Muffin Shoppe 8
Picket Fence Cafe 8
Crofton
Argo Hotel 9
Bogner's Steak House 10
Dakota City
Hungry's 11
David City
Thomas Tavern 11
Dixon
Euni's Palace.. 11
Fremont
Andy's on First.. 12
Carey Cottage 13
Fremont Dinner Train 14
Irv's Deli and More 15
Nick's on Main Street Grill.. 15
Hooper
Office Bar and Grill 16
Leshara
Longbranch 17
Martinsburg
Bob's Bar 18
Neligh
Daddy's Country Cafe 18
Imperial Steakhouse 19

Newman Grove
City Cafe 20
Hombre Steakhouse 20
Norfolk
Uptown Eating Establishment 20
Oakland
Corner Coffee Shop 22
Pierce
Cuthills Winery 23
Plainview
Grandma Carol's Bread Kitchen 24
Prague
Kolač Kafe 25
Royal
Green Gables 26
Schuyler
Husker Bar 28
Top Notch 28
Scribner
Scribner Hotel Restaurant 28
Stanton
Wolf's Den 29
Wahoo
Wigwam Cafe 29
OK Market 31
Wakefield
Jeanne's at the Haskell House 32
Wayne
Riley's 33
Wynot
Sportsman's Steakhouse and Lounge 33

SOUTHEAST

A Hairnet with Stars by Ted Kooser 36
Ulbrich's, Nebraska City by Robert Hanna 37
Ashland
Granny's Cafe 39
Kiewit Lodge, Mahoney State Park 39
Beatrice
Black Crow 39
Bennet
Mamasita's 41

Cedar Creek
Anna's Restaurant 42
Crete
Magic Wok 43
Dwight
Cy's.. 44
Emerald
Merle's Food and Drink 45
Fairbury
Sale Barn Cafe 46
Stable 46
Griffey's.. 46
Milford
Kup 'n Kettle.. 46
Nebraska City
Lied Conference Center 47
Teresa's Family Restaurant 48
Ulbrick's 48
Pawnee City
Hallie's 49
Pleasant Dale
Keller's II 50
PD Quick Shop.. 51
Porky's 51
Rulo
Camp Rulo 52
Seward
Peppercorn 52
Springfield
Springfield Drug 53
Steele City
Salty Dog.. 53
Tecumseh
Old Cafe 54

NORTH CENTRAL

Memo to Marge by Don Welch.. 56
Double T Cafe, Halsey by Robert Hanna 57
Ainsworth
Our Place 59
Anselmo
Smet's Cafe 59

Bassett
Range Cafe 60
Boelus
Golden Nugget 61
Brewster
Uncle Buck's 61
Broken Bow
Charlene's 63
Lobby Restaurant 63
Cairo
Tony's Restaurant 64
Dannebrog
Danish Baker 66
Harriett's Danish 67
Elba
Nila's 69
Elyria
Country Neighbor 69
Ericson
Hungry Horse Saloon 70
Gross
Nebraska Inn 71
Hyannis
Double J-T Cafe and Bar 72
Lynch
Bakery Cafe 72
Merriman
Bowring Ranch State Park 73
Naper
Naper Cafe 74
Ord
Diner 74
Rockville
Gin's Tavern 75
Seneca
Cattleman's Restaurant and Lounge 76
Taylor
Bridge Club 76
Thedford
Cowpoke Inn 76
Tryon
Sowders Ranch Store 77

Valentine

Jordan's 78

Peppermill 78

Ambrosia Gardens 79

Snake Falls Canyon Restaurant 79

SOUTH CENTRAL

Nebraska by Ron Hansen 82

Nifty Drive-In, Grand Island by Robert Hanna 83

Alda

Dowd's 85

Byron

Korner Kafe 85

Franklin

Brad's Supper Club 86

Grand Island

Coney Island Lunch Room 86

Dreisbach's 88

El Tapatio 89

Fourth Street Cafe 89

La Mexicana 90

Nonna's Palazzo 91

Edwardian Lady Tea Room & Curiosity Shop 93

Plum Thicket Tea Room & Gift Shop 93

Guide Rock

Plantation 93

Harvard

Black Dog Diner 94

Hastings

La Mejicana 94

Holdrege

Zephyr Cafe 95

Kearney

Alley Rose 95

Cellar 96

Downhome Gourmet 96

French Cafe 97

Habǝtat 97

Simply Desserts 99

Tex's Cafe 99

Minden

J and J's City Cafe 100

Osceola

CJ's 100

Republican City

Little Mexico 100

Strang

Jan's Strang Tavern 101

Stromsburg

Aunt Ruth's 102

Sutton

Big Idea Cafe 103

York

Chances R 104

SOUTHWEST

In the Cafe by Marjorie Saiser 106

Ole's Big Game Bar, Paxton by Robert Hanna 107

Cozad

Little Deuce Coupe 109

PJ's 109

Curtis

Yellow Rose 110

Eustis

Pool Hall 111

Hershey

Butch's Bar 112

Indianola

Rocket Inn 113

Lexington

Dotty's Diner 114

Leprechaun 114

North Platte

Brick Wall 115

Doris' Tavern 116

Ogallala

Cassel's Family Restaurant 117

Hilltop Inn 118

Homemade Heaven Sandwich Shop 118

Paxton

Ole's Big Game Lounge 119

Wellfleet

Country Inn 120

WEST

Breakfast at the Tunnel Inn by William Kloefkorn 122
Yellow Rose, Gering by Robert Hanna 123
Bayard
Oregon Trail Wagon Train 125
Bridgeport
Sweet Things Bakery 126
Chadron
Olde Main Street Inn 127
Gering
Bush's Gaslight 128
Giggling Gourmet 128
My Victorian Heart 129
Harrison
Sioux Sundries 129
Hemingford
Carol's Cafe 130
Kimball
Mi Ranchito 131
Lakeside
Cattlemen's 132
Lewellen
Vic's Steakhouse and Lounge 132
Lisco
Roost 133
Melbeta
Flame 133
Sidney
Dude's Steak House 134
Sanna's 135
Scottsbluff
El Charrito 136
Rosita's 137
Woodshed 138

LINCOLN

Lincoln by Hilda Raz 140
Tastee Inn, Lincoln by Robert Hanna 141
Barrymore's 143
Billy's 144

Blue Heron 145
Cookie Company 146
Cornhusker Hotel 147
Terrace Grille 147
The Renaissance 147
Crane River 148
Dem Bonz 149
El Mercadito 151
Four Suns 152
Garden Cafe 153
Green Gateau 153
Grottos 154
Imperial Palace 155
Inn Harm's Way 156
JaBrisco 156
K's Restaurant 157
Lazlo's 158
The Mill 159
Misty's 160
Moian's Bakery 161
The Oven 161
Papa John's 162
Piezano's 163
PO Pears 163
Rock 'N Roll Runza 164
The Steak House 165
Taste of India 166
Ted and Wally's 166
Valentino's 166
Vincenzo's 167
YiaYia's 168

OMAHA

Lunch at Jams Grill by Art Homer 170
The Old Market, Omaha by Robert Hanna 171
The Aquarium 173
Cafe de Paris 173
Claudia's 174
Empanada House 174
Flatiron 176
French Cafe 177
Garden Cafe 178

La Strada 72 179
M's Pub 180
Market Basket 181
Maxine's 182
Mister C's 182
Nettie's 183
Old Vienna Cafe 184
Spanna 184
Stella's 185
Ted and Wally's 186
V. Mertz 186
Vivace 187
Zio's 188

Barbecue Omaha
Jim's Rib Haven 189
Old Mill Barbecue 189
Skeet's 189

Ethnic Eateries
Afghani-Kabob 190
Ahmad's 190
Bohemian Cafe 191
Butsy LeDoux's 191
Chez Chong 192
El Alamo 192
Food Gallery 192
Greek Islands 193
H and I Cafe 193
Imperial Palace 194
Indian Oven 194
Jaipur 195

Neighborhood Italian
Frankie and Phyl's 196
Leonardo's Lo Sole Mio 196
Raphael's 197
Sons of Italy Hall 197
Villa Fiorita 197

Omaha Steakhouses
Angie's 199
Caniglia's 199
Gorat's 199
Johnny's 200
Omaha Prime 200
Ross' 200

CONDIMENTS

The M and L Cafe by Marjorie Saiser 202
Hotel Wilber, Wilber by Robert Hanna 203
My Favorite Dives 205
Driving Nebraska by Francis Moul 209
Dining on the MoPac East Trail by Richard Conradt 213
Eating Texas: Husker Fans Go South 216
My Favorite Place in Nebraska by Andrew Schultz 218
Cats in the Catsup 220

INDEX

Cafes 223
Cities 226
Contributors 227

Introduction

Our first book, *Eating Nebraska,* was published in 1990. Since the statute of limitations on food poisoning lawsuits has expired—and hopefully none of our readers have—we've dared to write a sequel, *Second Helpings: More Eating Nebraska.*

We also decided to write a second book because Nebraskans are hungry to learn about new places to eat. After watching Husker football and talking Husker football, eating may be the state's favorite pastime. If you don't agree with this, here's a little story that friends swear is true.

Before the opening of Mullen's world-class Sandhills Golf Course, the developers were eating lunch at a tavern in town. A local rancher sauntered up and asked if they were the ones building the new golf club south of town. He also asked how much it would cost to join. The surprised developers told him the price, which was more than enough to buy a small herd of cows and a very good bull. Unfazed, the rancher told them he was interested in signing up.

"You a golfer?" one developer asked. "Nope," the rancher replied. "Well, if you don't golf, why would you want to a join a golf club?" With a wry smile the rancher explained, "Always looking for a new place to eat around here."

So we offer you this book, *Second Helpings*, our latest attempt to scout out Nebraska's newest and most unique places for supper. *Second Helpings* is filled with current reviews of recent discoveries as well as all-new descriptions of your old favorites. The reviews—over 250—are new or revised based on dozens of food forays during the last few years. The format is familiar for readers of our first book, *Eating Nebraska.* We've highlighted unique dining spots in six regions of the state, plus Lincoln and Omaha. We've added new essays and new features. We're proud of Bob Hanna's wonderful illustrations and the cafe poems written by a score of Nebraska poets. In a special chapter, entitled Condiments, we added something a little extra to accompany your meals. Guest writers describe their memorable Nebraska destinations, and for the food-obsessed fans, we've recommended restaurants in the Texas cities of the Big Twelve Conference.

A lot of gustatory effort went into this research. We've eaten at more than 400 places, driven over 15,000 miles, and packed countless calories into these tummies. We've defied the health experts and food police who preach that every thing from fettuccine to fudge is bad for you. We think Julia Child has the right idea, "Food is fun, and if you don't have any fun, you might as well not be living."

It's true, we've picked up a few pounds, but we'd like to set the record straight. We categorically deny the rumor spread by some of Dick's schoolmates. He **does not** weigh three hundred pounds. And Katherine **does not** haul him from restaurant to cafe in the back of a cattle trailer . . . the back of our pickup is quite sufficient.

Just like *Eating Nebraska*, we highlight unique destinations—places that have a memorable quality and interesting atmosphere along with decent food. We've searched out great family-owned spots, out of the way taverns, and small-town cafes that pack them in. The so-called reviews are really descriptions, designed to help you choose a special place to eat. If we didn't like a place, it's not in the book. And if you find a special place not listed, we may not have discovered it yet. We're not food critics—we just like to explore Nebraska. And hope you do, too.

Also remember that even the best restaurants often disappear without a trace; others may have unpredictable hours. Unless you're the adventurous type, call ahead. Phone numbers are listed for each entry.

We encourage you to explore Nebraska. Drive the dusty back roads. Poke around the little towns with this book as your guide. You'll find extraordinary sights and friendly people; the food is a fringe benefit. If you follow our advice to wander off the beaten path, we promise that in addition to full tummies, you'll be filled with pleasure and drunk with delight at the discoveries you'll make. And if you can't hit the road, we hope that reading *Second Helpings* will make you feel as if you've been there.

Nebraska Wine

Tipping the bottle, pouring, twisting the drop
from the lip, the bottom half of the glass
filled molten gold, a hint of the light at play
in the tumble of tiny specklike bubbles,
like seeds through the skins of the slopeside grapes;
turned seedless, then, once settled; over the rim,
the nose at its work of savoring the bouquet;
and then the swirl around the glass, the nose
again, and then the swished first taste, the crush
against the palate, as if you took a cluster
in the sudden burst of a single grape;
all of one summer held here in a moment
come flooding forth, the taste buds' Indian summer,
the summary dream of this precarious vintage
harvested from among the neighboring cornfields
and the birds' sweet depredations, the ridicule
of the farmers' skepticism (how if a thing
has not been tried before, it's not worth trying);
breasting the current, bucking the flow of the grain
of the local wisdom, until the grapes
had swelled to maturation, glistening,
and gathered carefully had entered on
the process of their transformation, earned
this tasting's measure of the small clear bottle,
the label's understatement of its riches,
the glasses clinked above the meal at table,
the cork drawn clean as the moral of a fable.

—Roy Scheele

Northeast

Claus Tavern - Columbus.

Marilyn's Tea Room
Beemer

417 East 3rd Street
402-528-3282

Marilyn Schantz, owner, manager, waitress, and gourmet cook at Marilyn's Tea Room, seems to be able to do it all. For years now, Marilyn, with the help of her mother, has been a special beacon in Beemer. Her luncheon fare (she only serves lunch, but opens in the evening by appointment) includes chicken crepes, Cornish hen, Windsor pork chops, family-style baked ham and chicken, as well as daily specials. She makes everything from scratch, *including the soda crackers.*

Soups, delicious rolls, crepes, pies, and artful presentation take this lovely, homey restaurant into a class by itself. It may be Nebraska's oldest tearoom-style restaurant—a concept that Marilyn pioneered and sustained.

The place itself is charming. Located in a hundred-year-old Queen-Anne-style house built by town founder A. D. Beemer in 1886, the restaurant and a quilt shop occupy the first floor and Marilyn lives upstairs. The interior features lots of woodwork and cleverly arranged treasures. The scene reminds us of big holiday dinners at grandma's when mismatched tables for all the guests filled the living room because she didn't have a dining-room table big enough for everybody. Lace curtains and sunny south windows are appealing.

The clientele at Marilyn's is interesting as well. There are well-dressed women, local businessmen, and farmers in bib overalls, proof that you don't have to own a steakhouse to attract the whole range of Nebraska appetites.

This is one of Nebraska's hidden treasures. It's a little place, in a little town, where little things count. And to our way of thinking, nothing is more important.

3

Cafe on Main

Blair

1621 Washington

402-426-2311

While many restaurateurs try authentic restoration of older buildings, the owners of the Cafe on Main took another tack. In just six months of renovation, a drugstore built in 1894 emerged a post-modern cafe that looks straight out of L.A. This is the sort of spot where sophisticated patrons debate the merits of half-decaf/half-caf cappuccino or real caf cappuccino, or both. In L.A. the Cafe on Main would go unnoticed, but in Blair, it's a continual surprise.

The tin ceiling and brick walls have been decorated with whites, purples, and turquoise for a frenzied eclectic look. Open odd hours, from 8:30 a.m. to 3:30 p.m., the cafe serves atypical dishes made from scratch: herbed rainbow trout and couscous chicken. The salad varieties include teriyaki chicken Sausalito, cobb, seafood, and spinach. The burgers match the theme; they're called new wave burgers. In fact, one midwesterner, unaccustomed to such unusual fare, inquired if they served anything other than this oriental food.

The Cafe on Main certainly fits our one-of-a-kind criterion—it's uncommonly unique and a lot of fun.

Catering Catering

Blair

1818 Lincoln

402-426-3235

This Victorian *home* is *home* to great *home*made breads, pies, and gourmet dishes for lunch or to take *home*. Cinnamon and pecan rolls, hot out of the oven each morning, score points with anyone loving *home* cooking. It'll remind you of *home*. So how would we rate Catering Catering? We'd give it an unequivocal Yes! Yes!

Dusters

2804 13th St.
402-562-6488 or 402-564-8338

Max Gottberg had a love affair with cars. Our story begins in 1903 when he bought one of the first cars in Columbus. Soon this farm boy moved to town to sell cars. Then he dreamed of building a deluxe auto dealership, and in 1920, he spent the then-huge sum of $65,000 to construct a building for the Gottberg Automobile Company, which he operated until his death in 1944.

Mac Hull, owner of the company that markets locally made Dorothy Lynch salad dressings, had a dream too. He wanted to open one of the finest restaurants in the Midwest. Two years and quite a bit more than $65,000 later, Dusters was born in the renovated Gottberg building. Incidentally, the restaurant's namesake is the long coat worn for protection by early motorists.

The history of Dusters, the restaurant, makes an interesting tale, but the real story unfolds with a visit to this grand establishment. Mr. Hull has spared no expense in creating a remarkable dining experience. First, there's an impressive range of world-class entrees. When they're combined with an extraordinary wine list and polished, gracious service, you get big-city sophistication. Servers take orders first from the female members of your party; the meal is served from the left-hand side and removed from the right. The presentation and serving of wine follows the traditional ritual, and the staff is alert to a diner's every wish.

The food wins raves. Unique offerings include alligator, ostrich, buffalo, salmon, escargot, lamb, veal, seafood, and, of course, steaks. Hull, a preservationist in every sense of the word, is dedicated to using fresh Nebraska food products. The ostrich comes from a farm north of Columbus, the salmon from near Bellwood, and escargot (yep, snails) will soon be raised in the area. Of course, beef, lamb, and pork are Nebraska specialties.

A 35-foot mural depicting two centuries of Nebraska history dominates the first-floor dining room. The atmosphere is slightly formal, but comfortable. A good match for the food.

The Gottberg Brew Pub is more informal. Separate from the dining room, but still on the main floor, it lets you see where the beer is made. Look behind the bar. There's a huge metal grain bin, a tribute to beer's origins. Close by is a labyrinth of tanks and pipes behind glass, an on-the-premises brewery. They make six different brews right there, plus the occasional special; try them all. Details are in the menu.

Max Gottberg's dream came true, and it looks like Mac Hull's will, too, because selling a good product and emphasizing service satisfy customers. Dusters is a Nebraska gem. It not only hits all the right culinary buttons, it pops a few, too. Stay tuned for the rest of this wonderful story.

Glur's Tavern *2301 11th St.*
Columbus *402-564-8615*

When you walk into Glur's Tavern, you step back in time. Glur's is the oldest continuously operating tavern west of the Missouri River—for real. Its claim was uncontested in a national competition sponsored by a beverage trade magazine.

Back in 1876 two Swiss immigrant brothers, Joseph and William Bucher, built what was then called the Bucher Saloon. An early helper in the saloon was the young Louis Glur who purchased it in 1914. The Glur family operated it up until a few years ago. Now the owners are a young couple, Carrie and Todd Trofholz. Todd grew up in Columbus and appreciates the history of the place.

William F. Cody, western scout, promoter, and notorious creator of Buffalo Bill's Wild West Show, visited the tavern in 1883. He had camped east of Columbus for several weeks rehearsing his show before a world tour. Legend has it that he laid a thousand dollar bill on the bar to buy a round of drinks for his performers and roustabouts. The poor owner is said to have fainted away.

The wooden, two-story building is located on the edge of downtown Columbus. The spacious bar and dining area are filled with old wooden tables and chairs. Often locals gather to play cards and chew the fat, so don't be surprised by the lively games going on around you. There's room for everyone at Glur's.

The fare is traditional American grub—soup and burgers. A beer garden in the rear allows patrons to play basketball, volleyball, or horseshoes in warm weather. Glur's Tavern is also the final destination for an annual ten-kilometer road race—the Columbus Downtown Runaround. City boosters serve pizza and pop to all comers, and those with a serious thirst head to the tavern for a great party.

Glur's Tavern is listed on the National Register of Historic Places, and it continues a long tradition of treating its customers well and seeing to it that they have a good time. Here's hoping it's around a hundred years from now.

Muffin Shoppe

Columbus

2905 14th St.
402-563-3333

A great luncheon spot for light, gourmet meals—delicious salads, soups, and sandwiches, and unusual specials, including quiches and decadent desserts. Popular with the ladies who lunch crowd, but men will savor it, too. In a restored house on a shady residential street. There's a delightful deck in back for pleasant summertime meals. Try to get a table back there. Attached is a gift shop for browsing before and after your meals.

Picket Fence Cafe

Columbus

2714 13th St.
402-563-3915

"Hey Mary Ann, be sure to save me a piece of that strawberry pie." When those are the first words you hear from a cafe regular, you know you've come to the right place. The fresh-baked pie at the Picket Fence won't last long; remember to order it first.

We followed the customer's lead and reserved our coconut cream and apple pies before ordering our entrees, home-made vegetable soup and gourmet sandwiches. Our Reuben was great, but there were lots of interesting sandwiches available.

May we tempt you with a few? How about hot shaved turkey, corned beef, and Swiss cheese on a grilled croissant with special dressing? Or try sliced roast beef smothered in Swiss cheese served on grilled marbled bread with grilled onions. The Monte Cristo sandwich has its own twist—shaved ham and turkey, melted Swiss and cheddar cheese, batter dipped, grilled and dusted with powdered sugar. The chicken Waldorf salad, made from chunks of chicken breast, celery, sweet pickle, walnuts, apples, and raisins, served with leaf lettuce on a lightly grilled croissant, is one of the lighter items. A super-duper BLT is the deluxe, three-cheese sandwich with tomato and bacon between melted cheeses on grilled rye. For seekers of still lighter fare, there are salads with homemade dressing. We liked the sea side salad—lettuce and other greens, lots of shrimp and crab, topped with cheddar cheese, egg, and tomatoes. Whew!

Frankly, after eating any of these, we doubt you'll have room for your pie.

Argo Hotel   *402-388-2400*
Crofton

This little hotel might be just the place to unwind after a stressful workweek. After several decades of operation as a health facility, the hotel now appeals to anyone seeking a hideaway off the beaten path. The Argo Hotel of Crofton, an elegantly restored property, was built in 1912 by Nick Michaelis. Named after the ship on which he came to America, it operated for a few years as the sole hotel in the town. Then in 1923, it was converted into the New Meridian Sanitarium, a facility emphasizing natural healing. For the next thirty years, it served as a doctor's office. After sitting empty, it took on new life when a Crofton family decided to reclaim its splendor. Now its charm heals the spirit.

As you enter the lobby you'll notice the original wide oak staircase and ornate tin ceiling. The carpet, a rich burgundy, complements the wood. Gleaming brass chandeliers and wall sconces with teardrop bulbs reflect in the brass and mirrors of the lobby. Nineteen restored rooms are available for guests.

When we stopped by, the dining room was not yet open for dinner, but we've had reports that they are now serving a limited menu. Included with the entree is a salad, relish tray, choice of potato, and hot, fresh bread. Plus live piano music! Hermenia Bogner, the 85-year-old mother of the hotel's proprietors, also known as the lady with the hat, plays in the evenings Sunday through Thursday.

Located near Lewis and Clark Lake, the town of Crofton bills itself as "the best little town by a dam site." The Argo Hotel may be Nebraska's best restored hotel site by dam! The Knox County hills beckon; this would be a great destination for a weekend getaway, especially in fall. For romantics, the manager will order flowers for your room, and be sure to request the honeymoon suite, complete with four-poster bed *and* a whirlpool bath. Those tempting amenities could restore the weariest traveler.

Bogner's Steak House
Crofton   *402-388-4626*

How can we explain the success of one of Nebraska's largest and best-known steakhouses—Bogner's in Crofton? It can't be location, as Crofton is miles from any of the big population centers, but if you give customers what they want—and what they want in a restaurant is consistently good food—they will come.

Forty years ago Bogner's was a small-town cafe reclaimed from the ruins of an abandoned gas station. Now the building looks cobbled together as one addition after another was built to accommodate its popularity.

The menu has amazing variety: crab legs, flaming escargot, and tender, sizzling, Nebraska steaks. The problem is that before you get to the entrees, you have to go through a salad bar that may be as extensive as any in the state. If plates were trucks, patrons would be cited for load violations.

On almost any night this place packs them in, a good indication of crowd-pleasing quality at a fair price.

Hungry's
Dakota City

100 No. 14th
402-987-3717

You won't go hungry at Hungry's. For the last nineteen years, this steakhouse has staked a claim to the business of serious beef-eating in extreme northeastern Nebraska. The specialty is charbroiled steaks cooked over an open grill in the dining room. You coach the cook on just the way you like it. The cottage-fried potatoes are also generous and special. There's even free ice cream to top off lunch.

Thomas Tavern
David City

536 5th St.
402-367-3021

This is a tavern so well known in the area it doesn't have a sign. Thomases have run the place continuously since 1888. Highlights are onion rings and greasy burgers cooked on an old cast-iron grill, known for miles around as Thomas burgers. Seems that this small-town tavern knows how to do good advertising by mouth.

Euni's Palace
Dixon

402-584-9309

Euni is obviously the star of this place—after all, it's her place. She serves up good food with a big smile. Pizza and burgers are her features. There are also noon specials. The last time we were there, she served up a huge, hot roast beef sandwich, fruit salad, and cherry pie. It was remarkably good, and at the remarkably low price of four bucks.

While you're in the Dixon area, a visit to the Tarbox Hollow Buffalo Ranch is a must. Euni, or anyone else in Dixon, can give you directions (it's northeast of town). Tours are available from May through September. The Mason family will take you out amongst these beasts of the Plains. You'll even get to feed them out of your hand—from the safety of an enclosed wagon. The tour is fun and educational.

Andy's on First
Fremont

102 N. Main St.
402-721-7474

Our favorite getaway in Fremont is an Italian cafe run by a colorful character, Chicago-transplant Andy Manes. Andy is an old-style restaurateur. A wiry, high-energy fellow whose caricature graces the front of the menu, Andy is friendly, funny, and seemingly everywhere at once. He loves entertaining his customers, serving good food, and hunting, in that order. His back room is a paean to the outdoor life and a certain black Labrador retriever—not what you'd expect to find in an Italian joint. Since Andy is nearly always at the restaurant, we figure he ought to be able to enjoy his pastime, if only on the wall.

We like his inventive specials, which he rarely repeats within the year. Pasta dishes come with a variety of sauces. The "No Name #1" is especially good—Italian sausage and chicken strips in roasted sweet pepper sauce served with mostaccioli. Baked entrees, such as lasagna, manicotti, and cannelloni, will satisfy the heartiest appetite. Andy's also serves seafood, veal, chicken, sandwiches, and pizzas. Good breads and unique starters complement the meal while Italian desserts finish it off. You can enjoy an expansive wine list and a variety of beers from micro-breweries.

You'll find Andy's on Fremont's main drag, but at the far south end, just before the tracks. In his corner location, he's created a wonderful, Chicago-style, neighborhood trattoria serving good Italian food and fun.

Carey Cottage
Fremont

732 Park Ave.
402-721-7640

Collectors of artifacts and antiquities flock to Fremont, the antique capital of eastern Nebraska. For determined collectors who want to see it all, Carey Cottage is there when the feet give out. This bright luncheon destination is exactly what Fremont needs to complement its convenient downtown antique shops.

Located just two steps from downtown in a little white house with an attractive courtyard, Carey Cottage serves luncheons to a mixed group of shoppers and business types. Open for an extended lunch hour Monday through Saturday, this charming teahouse serves mostly luncheon fare. Think soups, salads, sandwiches, light entrees, and desserts. Its signature is an appetizer course for every diner, served proudly on dark green depression glass. They also serve an afternoon tea accompanied by cakes, pastries, pies, and biscuits. You may want to make a reservation.

We enjoyed our time at Carey Cottage. Lunch was served expertly by friendly servers, despite Chautauqua crowds and hundred-degree temperatures outside. We felt soothed and pampered in its cool decor of white and green. An Irish

Victorian theme—antiques, dried flowers, and lace—decorates the cottage. The ornate powder room goes a bit over the top, almost too pretty to use. There's a lot to see in each of several dining rooms, and since the menus change frequently, you can go back again and again.

Fremont Dinner Train

Fremont

650 No. H St.
402-727-8321

Few Nebraska restaurants offer a view. Far fewer offer a moving view. But you get both when you hop aboard the Fremont Dinner Train. Granted, this isn't the California Zephyr steaming through the Rockies, but the Elkhorn Valley does have pastoral beauty that sets the perfect mood for combining a trip and dinner. Since you're not really going anywhere—except to Hooper and back—you can just relax and let the world go by. Enjoy the scenery and be mesmerized by the clickety-clack sounds of the past. You're doing something very unusual—nowhere else in the world is a dinner train pulled by a steam locomotive.

You will travel in the style and elegance of railroad travel fifty to seventy-five years ago. The interiors of the cars have been beautifully restored. There are plush red carpets, curtains, and oak woodwork. The music is vintage—Dorsey, Miller, and Ellington.

Friday and Saturday nights feature five-course meals served on crisp, white tablecloths and heavy, railroad china. Lighter three-course meals are offered on Sunday. The food is good and the menu varies. The entrees might be prime rib, Cornish game hen, salmon, quail, orange roughy, or steak.

If you want a little more activity, there are specialty runs, such as murder mystery trains or bingo trips. This is the essence of authentic 1940s rail travel. Whether you want to experience a train trip for first time or relive fond memories of railroad's golden age, climb aboard the Fremont and Elkhorn Valley Railroad.

Irv's Deli and More

35 West 6th St.

Fremont

402-721-2015

Irv's is a New York delicatessen that took a wrong turn and found itself in Fremont. Great sandwiches and deli sides rank right up there with the best of New York City—places like the Carnegie Delicatessen or the 2nd Avenue Deli. It's a ranking that Irv's deserves.

Nick's on Main Street Grill

439 No. Main St.

Fremont

402-727-9600

We've eaten in this little grill on two occasions and both times we've been impressed with the inventive menu. It's definitely a hole-in-the-wall. From the outside you see a plain, small-town bar and basically, that's what you'll find inside. They've stuck some eclectic stuff on the walls to slick it up, but the facilities definitely have not kept up with the menu. The draw here is the wide variety of intriguing food— there's truly something for every appetite. Nick's also has a micro-brewed beer on tap if you want to try something different to drink.

Beef eaters will go for the prime rib or a burger variation. The nostalgic can tie into liver and onions. You'll find an array of lighter entrees, including a stir-fry dish. Dark, chunky steak soup and French onion soup are served with great rolls. A bowl of soup could be a meal in itself. We sampled a delicious, lemon pepper catfish, not heavy or breaded. Rice pilaf and lightly steamed baby carrots accompanied the dish. The special was filet New Orleans, a seafood-stuffed filet, blackened and served with peppery sauce. The Reuben sandwich was the original and as good as it gets.

Locals still complain that Nick's has done away with its taco special on Monday nights. Others will tell you that the food quality varies. We think it's worth a try, and if you can't find something to enjoy on this menu, you're too picky to complain.

The Office Bar and Grill   *402-654-3373*
Hooper

The Office Bar and Grill resides in the best-preserved restaurant building on the best-preserved main street in Nebraska. The west side of Hooper's main drag remains just the way it was one hundred years ago. The street is lined with nine brick buildings in the American Renaissance style of architecture. (For you architectural buffs, there are also elements of Romanesque revival and Italianate.) The buildings have survived because the town council required that all new buildings be built of brick after a devastating fire in the 1880s. Recognizing the treasure in their midst, Hooperites have refused to alter these buildings. The whole west side of main street is now included on the National Register of Historic Places. Adding charm to the buildings is a continuous tin awning that covers the sidewalk on the north end of the row. The original wooden benches lining the sidewalk have been worn slick by generations of overall-covered backsides.

One of the most interesting buildings is the one that houses the Office. Once inside, you realize that everything about these stately old buildings has been preserved. Original wood floors and pressed-tin ceiling remain. The walls are decorated with antiques, including the old Hooper High clock and a collection of Hooper High pennants.

The food is better than bar fare. We were there for lunch and the Office was packed. The hot roast beef sandwiches were excellent, and we'll long remember the coconut cream pie topped with a full four inches of meringue.

Those who have taken the excursion train from Fremont to Hooper have undoubtedly discovered the Office. It's a find, not only because of its historic significance, but because it is simply a comfortable, friendly place to have a beer or enjoy some good food.

Longbranch
Leshara

402-721-8882

The Longbranch is a place you'd see in western films. It's the kind of saloon where during the big bar fight, one hombre is thrown into the street through the front window and the marshal chases a rustler who gets away by leaping from rooftop to the back of a horse. You get the picture. In fact, all that really happened at the Longbranch. Fortunately, it was staged; a barroom brawl was filmed here several years ago. At the turn of the century, however, the Branch didn't have to stage its brawls. Look up at the one hundred-year-old ceiling; those are real bullet holes.

Civilization and a measure of decorum have tamed the Longbranch. The wildest thing now is when Jimmi Prentiss' one-person band leads the Saturday night sing-alongs.

Popular menu items are prime rib (claimed to be the "best prime rib anywhere"), homemade soup, and a salad bar highlighted by homemade bread. The Longbranch is a friendly place to whoop it up on Saturday night. But save the ceiling; check your six-shooters at the door.

Bob's Bar
Martinsburg
402-945-2995

If you're squeamish or a neat freak, Bob's Bar is not for you. It sits smack dab on the evolutionary scale somewhere between a joint and a dive, but folks in the area recommend it as a novelty. If you're feeling adventuresome and accept a little dust and grease in a small-town bar, try Bob's. Granted, your first reaction might be to wonder whether they serve food in such a place, but after the initial shock, order the burger and fries. The giant burger overwhelms the crusty bun and satisfies the heartiest appetite. If you're shy of the food, have a beer—it's bottled.

Daddy's Country Cafe
Neligh
402-887-5500

Check out the cheery atmosphere at Daddy's Country Cafe, a great place to go for your first cup of coffee in the morning. If the caffeine won't do the trick, the bright, country surroundings will. Blue gingham checks and sunflowers create a cheery, blue-and-yellow theme. Stencils on the wall and little red hearts could make even the grumpiest grin. Patrons donate hats to an ever-growing collection and flock to the cafe for chicken-fried steak with real mashed potatoes and gravy. The sour cream raisin pie deserves mention. We were stuffed from over-the-road food foraging when we paid the cafe a visit. Even without appetites, we found goodies to nibble on and bright friendly faces to greet us. Daddy's Country Cafe still makes us smile.

Imperial Steakhouse

Neligh

The question of the day at the Newman Grove sex education class was, "How far do you think you should go on your first date?" Without hesitating, the eighth-grade boy answered, "I'd probably go all the way to Neligh."

That's the same answer many area residents give because they want to go to the Imperial Steakhouse in Neligh—a one-business enterprise zone including dining room, lounge, deli, and package liquor store.

The Imperial is an excellent Nebraska steakhouse. The soup is particularly good. Besides steak, the Imperial makes a stab at seafood and sandwiches. The most unique feature, however, is next door in the adjoining lounge known as the Imperial Gallery. The lounge was built as a livery stable in 1903. The original beams and brick walls were preserved; even the metal rings used to tie horses are attached to the walls. The bricks and copper tabletops create a cozy feeling in the room.

The dining room takes another tack. Its focal point is—a tree trunk—plain and bare. Maybe Nebraskans are starved for the forest. This is not the first tree we've spotted in our travels to eateries around the state, but the raison d'tree fails to take root. Anyway, the food is good, and we suspect that a Saturday night could be pretty lively in the old livery.

City Cafe

402-447-6446

Hombre Steakhouse

402-447-9432

Newman Grove

This comfy cafe serves the most unusual sauerkraut in Nebraska. The cafe's owner and cook, Phyllis Weitzel, describes it as sweetened sauerkraut. It's certainly an oxymoron, but a scrumptious one. It passed the customer test— they tried it, they liked it. Now Phyllis says she can't make enough of it for her popular Sunday buffet, an all-you-can-eat affair at a very modest price.

We were there on a cold Saturday noon and enjoyed the hot beef sandwich special accompanied by another unusual concoction, spicy french fries. The homemade apple pie fortified us for a successful afternoon of pheasant hunting with the local banker, Jeff Gerhart, a hunting and eating aficionado.

Down the street from the City Cafe is the Hombre Steakhouse, a place to get serious about Nebraska steaks in a light-hearted, south-of-the-border atmosphere. The Mexican motif is set off with strings of little lights, reminiscent of the Christmas-year-round atmosphere of Mister C's in Omaha. It's a great place to celebrate after a long day of hunting.

The Uptown Eating Establishment

326 Norfolk Ave.

Norfolk

402-371-7171

The Uptown Eating Establishment is the hands-down winner for choice dining in Norfolk. The winner of six international food awards, including the Gourmet Diner's Silver Spoon Award, the AAA three-diamond award, and dozens of area awards, the Uptown uses only the finest, whole, natural ingredients. The chefs avoid all the no-no's of fine cuisine—canned, pre-cooked, or processed items; convenience or gimmick; refined sugar and salt. Instead, they stress natural ingredients, such as honey and maple syrup, nut and seed oils, authentic Japanese tamari, a variety of beans, seeds, grains, and spices. They are attentive even to minute details, such as the ratio of sodium to potassium.

The Uptown is located downtown in the historic, old Kensington-Norfolk Hotel. The five-story landmark has been renovated and includes the original grand ballroom and the hotel dining area that is now occupied by the Uptown.

The decor of the restaurant is classy forties art deco. The main dining room looks like a room out of a Bogart film—black booths, southwestern pastels of peach and bronze, large planters, lazy ceiling fans straight out of Casablanca, and artful accessories arranged around the room. It has a dark, sophisticated feel, a far cry from the way it must have looked when Norfolk native Johnny Carson did his first radio show in this very room.

The most unique thing about the Uptown is its innovative food. The starters include elegant appetizers: salmon mousse, cool and creamy with a hint of dill; herring à la Russe, herring marinated in cream wine sauce; golden caviar, fresh white-fish caviar with whipped cream cheese; beef terrine, a silky pate of prime beef with rye toast.

The entrees are just as exotic. Here's a sample of the incredible variety: steak Johannesburg, tenderloin filet sauteed in butter with crab, shrimp, and other seafoods, topped with Madeira cream sauce; salmon steak with crabmeat creole sauce; trout, locally grown; swordfish, not locally grown, but cooked with fumet of lobster cream. It goes on and on. Special selections by the chef are featured and may include venison, pheasant, or perhaps, beef Wellington.

Corner Coffee Shop
Oakland

402-685-5223

There's a bit of Sweden nestled in the hills of northeast Nebraska. Oakland has proclaimed itself the Swedish capital of Nebraska. Neighboring Swedes and townsfolk swear allegiance to a little local spot that may be nearly as old as the town itself—the Corner Coffee Shop.

Locals say that the Corner Coffee Shop has been there for most of the 125+ years that Oakland has been on the map. Just a half block from the railroad tracks, it was a long-ago watering hole for train passengers waiting for locomotives to take on water and fuel. In the heyday of train travel, the coffee shop was open twenty-four hours a day, seven days a week.

It's still popular today as a downtown gathering place, although its hours are cut back just a bit. When we last visited, it was crowded in mid-morning. The old wooden floor was worn smooth from years of use. The counter was full of farmers and townsfolk perched on the wooden stools with their feet resting on the iron rail below. Lively conversation accompanied serious eating.

The Corner Coffee Shop prepares hearty cafe fare, satisfying on its own, but for us the treat has always been the delicious, sweet, Swedish rye bread. We like to take it home to toast and eat with homemade jam. They don't promote bread sales by the loaf. We had to talk them into it. So to avoid the disappointment of finding the bread sold out, call ahead to reserve your loaf so you can take home a delicious Swedish souvenir.

And while in Oakland, drive around the pretty little town. There are decorated storefronts and signs in Swedish and flowers in summertime. On corner lampposts you'll find a herd of the ubiquitous red rocking horse, a Swedish folk symbol.

And if you're a real Swedish aficionado, you'll come back for the annual Swedish festival. Just be sure to reserve some time at the Corner Coffee Shop.

Cuthills Winery   *402-329-6774*
Pierce

When it comes to agriculture, Nebraskans find ways to innovate, figuring a way to scratch a living from the land one way or another. With crossbred cattle, hybrid corn, center pivots, and enormous, round hay bales replacing the small, square backbusters of youth, Nebraskans adapt to new times. Old farmers may think they've seen it all, but maybe not yet. Now there's even a winery in a climate thought too harsh to grow grapes.

You have to be creative and a bit stubborn to grow grapes in Nebraska. Holly and Ed Swanson are stubborn. But the combination of stubbornness, creativity, and hard work has paid off. They do grow grapes in Nebraska, and they do produce fine Nebraska wine. They've created a gift for Nebraskans—the Cuthills Winery—Nebraska's first and only winery.

In the Midwest we've tasted several abortive attempts to create wine. There are small wineries in Missouri and Kansas. Unfortunately, their wines have the appeal of a spent glass of champagne. The Cuthills wines, however, are fragrant, cool, and dancing.

The Cuthills Winery is located on fifteen acres in the hills two miles west of Pierce. Locally these hills are known as the cuthills, a place where ancient glaciers cut through the soil. It's a pretty drive and worth the time to see how grapes are grown and wine is made—and to bring home several bottles of very good native wine. You can tour the vineyards, wander through the weathered 1927 barn where the wines are produced, and pick from a variety of wines in the tasting room. For example, they have a crisp and delicious white wine made from the LaCrosse grape; a light, dry, fruity red wine with subtle hints of cherry; mead, a very mild and lightly sweet wine made from Nebraska honey; and fruit wines made from apple and blueberry.

The Swansons are not only stubborn and creative, they're talented and experienced, having made wine for sixteen years. These traits are reflected in the wines they produce. Give this brave little winery a try, even if you've never tried wine before.

Grandma Carol's Bread Kitchen   *402-582-4441*
Plainview

Through the screen door of Grandma Carol's, a view of the kitchen and the unmistakable aroma of fresh-baked bread transport you to a bygone era. Grandma Carol's *is* grandma's house. There is an antique dough cupboard next to a Hoosier cabinet, old rocking chairs and tables, and a woman who knows cooking, and loves to see people enjoy her offerings.

Grandma Carol's will seduce you with the sensual sights, sounds, and smells of real home cooking. In fact, you can sit in the middle of it, just as you used to sit at grandma's dining table eating cookies and watching her roll dough for a pie. At Grandma Carol's, the dining room is near the kitchen so you can watch her work her miracles with dough and pie crust. See Grandma Carol slide her unbaked bread into the classic blue cookstove. Watch steaming fruit pies emerge, extracted by hot pad-covered hands. It's the best place in the world to play hookey from adult responsibility.

But like being at grandma's, you occasionally have to pitch in. You find your own seats, pour your own drinks, and dish up your own food once in a while. Of course, there's no cash register. You're trusted to figure up your own bill, and put money into quart milk bottles placed on each table. If you need change, you make your own from an antique bill changer near the entrance. And there's one more thing, just like at grandma's, you have to take the dishes to the sink.

Carol Hall, the one-woman baker/cook/manager, serves great rolls and muffins for breakfast and features two main dishes for lunch each day. Some of her favorite offerings are lasagna, assorted sandwiches made with homemade buns or bread, salads, sour cream raisin pie, and strawberry pizza. She closes in the evenings and on Sundays.

Sometime we're going to show up for breakfast, then hunker down in the two rocking chairs to watch, smell, and hear the cooking show. At noon we'll move, of course, to a table for lunch. After lunch, all we'll need is a place for a nap.

Kolač Kafe
Prague   402-663-4869

The huge Kolač Kafe was nearly empty the morning we stopped by. There were only seventeen people enjoying their morning coffee break! We saw the local priest, neighbor women talking about their gardens, farmers predicting their best-ever crops, and a table of mothers and daughters spanning three generations. The bakery case held dozens of kolaches, at least six varieties, but we had a feeling they'd be gone before the place closed. It was only 9:30 a.m. and the luncheon special hadn't yet been announced. The cook was feeling a little churlish and hadn't made up his mind. Nope, we'd missed the famous pork sandwiches; they were served the day before. When would they be served again? Nobody knew.

There's a Friday night fish fry and a noon special on Sundays. On Friday the place turns into a beer hall, too, with drinks served in a room on the side.

Don't miss this Czech social club in Prague, a tiny community on the edge of the Bohemian Alps. Visit the Czechland Recreation Area north of town and notice the wonderful European-style barn located just across the road to the east. Prague is a community stuck in time, and it's not a bad place to be.

Green Gables   402-893-5800
Royal

Old animals are responsible for the success of Green Gables. Really old animals—ten-million-year-old animals—uncovered at Ashfall Fossil Beds bring hundreds of tourists to this part of northeast Nebraska. Ashfall Fossil Beds, a fascinating archeological dig and prehistoric site, has been described as sitting out in the middle of nowhere. It almost goes without saying that there was nowhere to eat out there. The owners of Green Gables, showing Nebraska ingenuity, moved an old barn two miles and rebuilt it on the route to Ashfall. Now tourists coming to look at the three-toed horses, rhinos, and camels have a good place to eat before and after their visit.

Green Gables is so closely tied to Ashfall that their seasons correspond. They're both open seven days a week from Memorial Day Weekend through Labor Day. After Labor Day, hours are limited and, in fact, the place is closed for a couple of months after December 31.

The dark burgundy barn sports gables that are, of course, green. The burgundy-and-green theme continues inside to create a comfortable, rural atmosphere. Barn siding covers one wall, and a restored banister from an old home in the area leads to the loft. Antiques and old pictures on the wall complete the decor. Long harvest tables covered with colorful oilcloth provide the seating. The tables were filled for lunch on the weekend we were there.

A mother-daughter team, Lois Dempster and Denise Hartigan, own the restaurant and do a great job producing hearty meals—the kind that used to be served to threshing crews on the farm. There's broasted chicken, roast beef, all kinds of sandwiches, and the specialty of the house, homemade pies. Rhubarb pie in season is the one to order, made just the way it should be. The owners describe all their pies as "baked fresh every morning in our kitchen, with lard in the pie crust and lots of calories to make them nice and rich. Definitely not for the diet-conscious customer." You just diet when you get home.

The good food and comfortable surroundings of Green Gables will bring you back to the twentieth century after an engrossing visit to this interesting site. You can work up an appetite viewing some very old bones. At Green Gables the only bones you'll find are those leftover.

Husker Bar

402-352-9980

Schuyler

At noon the biggest restaurant in Schuyler is a bar--the Husker Bar. Its bare-bones decor of mismatched tables, chairs, and dinnerware, and simple, hearty cooking reflect the true spirit of "cheap eats." When we were there, the half-size dinner, the size of the full dinner at most places, was $1.75. You'll see men in ties, ladies who lunch, farmers in overalls, construction workers, secretaries, and mechanics. It attracts everyone who likes to eat a lot for a little.

Top Notch

402-352-5110

Schuyler

This is a typical main street cafe with cooking good enough to keep it on the main street. We tried the Top Notch and found it just fine. The vegetable barley soup was the genuine article with a rich, dark broth and big chunks of vegetable. The marinated chicken swimming in barbecue sauce was inventive, and the peach pie divine. The dining room was once the Schuyler post office (1907). The food wasn't fancy, but neither are we. That's why this ex-post office cafe is good enough to write home about.

Scribner Hotel Restaurant

402-664-2462

Scribner

This relic hotel in downtown Scribner (built in 1901 and included on the National Register of Historic Places) teases the appetites of Scribnerites with cosmopolitan dishes like crab and shrimp pasta. Manager Paulette Cooley has been cooking since she was ten, and we think she's got it right.

Wolf's Den

Stanton

402-439-2128

We drove to Stanton to check out a couple of spots only to find that they'd closed down. Disappointed, and admittedly a bit hungry, we drove around town looking for sustenance. Finally we spied a blue-and-white building with an old-fashioned canvas awning and a sign that puffed Lynette's Great Home Cookin Since 1981. The owner of the Wolf's Den, a lonely survivor in Stanton, had the confidence to claim she could cook. With empty stomachs, that was good enough for us.

Curtained windows and the dim light of beer signs did create a den-like atmosphere. As our eyes adjusted to the darkness, we noticed the interesting dark-wood ceiling, dark pillars, and huge old back bar. But more important, we noticed dishes of pickle and onion on each table and women cooking up luncheon specials in the back.

We were saved from starvation with the Wolf's Den's special of the day—pork chop, corn, mashed potatoes, stuffing, bread and butter, and strawberry shortcake for $4.50. It was a delicious meal at a most gentle price. Lynette *can* cook. We hope she continues to thrive in the Wolf's Den. She'll tame the most ferocious appetite.

Wigwam Cafe

Wahoo

146 East 5th
402-443-5575

Welcome back to the Wigwam, a quintessential small-town cafe and legendary eatery, first opened in 1932. The threat of losing this familiar landmark brought sadness to folks in Wahoo. People in this community know what it's like to lose a friendly cafe. Six years after Wahoo's famous Fairview

29

Cafe closed, townspeople and travelers still mourn its passing. When the Wigwam was put up for sale, the locals were not optimistic. But fate has a way of finding a solution. In this case, love and marriage gave the Wigwam a new lease on life. A happy, new beginning all the way around.

New owners, Silvia and Clayton Wade, made a big commitment. Not yet married, they fell in love with the Wigwam on a visit to meet Clayton's parents. Silvia, a Hungarian born in Romania, had always wanted to operate a cafe. The Wigwam presented itself, they signed the papers, and that sealed the Wades' business and marital collaboration. In fact, the couple married in the cafe and spent their honeymoon working there.

Our visit to the Wigwam included longtime area residents Rosalie and Louis Noha with their oldest daughter, Margaret Berry, now a Lincoln resident. The family reminisced about the cafe and their lives in the Wahoo area while we enjoyed a great meal and inviting atmosphere.

Hands down, you can't beat the food. The special was a breaded chicken tenderloin with to-die-for real mashed potatoes seasoned with onions and dill, and excellent green beans with baby carrots. The Wigwam remembers vegetables! The chicken was served with fiery dipping sauce that tasted of catsup, brown sugar, and a hot pepper sauce. Sandwich fare includes the usual variety, but a special offering that day was the Rachel—the Wigwam version of a turkey Reuben. Homemade soup (chicken vegetable) and coleslaw (also yummy with pineapple and dill) accompanied our meals. We were well satisfied. Prices are modest.

The surroundings are a nostalgic dark green and burgundy; the Nohas say the back bar has always been painted green. Picture 1940s decor—soda fountain, stools, booths, brick walls, and tile. The decorations favor a Native American motif; the brown tepee-shaped sign out front is a classic.

Open every day from early morning until mid-afternoon, the Wigwam is the destination of choice in Wahoo. Townspeople are happy. Travelers are happy. Thanks to the wonderful young Wades and the Wigwam. We hope they live happily ever after.

OK Market
Wahoo

542 Linden
402-443-3015

The OK Market is a temple to the hot dog—frankfurters, wieners, and sausages—and a shrine to childhood memories. You can buy anything they can stuff into a natural casing and link together—the old-fashioned way. It's the same way it was done when the OK Market opened in 1919. The wieners are done up in all forms, classic and otherwise: long and thin, big and thick, short and stubby. There's standard ground, coarsely ground, laced with spice, laced with garlic, Polish sausage, cream sausage, and potato sausage. The last time we checked, they had twenty-three different recipes, all variations on the wiener theme.

The OK Market itself is a classic. Using a 1920s picture as a guide, the owner completely restored the market. The interior is a two-tone brown, almost the color of the wieners. And on the outside, the faded green, oval meat sign has been left just as it was.

The OK Market is not a restaurant. It's a wiener market. You select whatever wieners you want out of the deli case, pack a cooler you have brought along for the occasion, and take them home. For weeks you'll enjoy the best wieners in the Midwest. Like thoughts of baseball games and family picnics, they'll make you smile.

Jeanne's at the Haskell House
Wakefield

320 Johnson St.
402-287-2587

Diners in northeast Nebraska have a treat in their midst. Wakefield is lucky enough to have one of the finest restaurants in Nebraska. We had more recommendations about this restaurant than any other in the state, and we were thrilled that it lived up to its billing. Be advised: it's not a good choice for burgers and beer. This is a sophisticated, elegant restaurant proudly bringing you big-city specialties.

The lovely setting complements the meals served here. The Haskell House is a restored, historic home. No expense was spared to create a unique atmosphere. The grounds have been landscaped with rose arbors and beautiful perennials. An enormous glass conservatory in the Victorian style has been added in back, and it holds the most desirable seats in the house, especially at sundown when the garden lights showcase the magnificent restoration.

What might you find on a typical night? There are always specials. Our choices were chicken Gorgonzola—a cheesy sauce on fettuccine; salmon framboise—salmon filets on rice with a berry sauce; beef tournedos with peppercorn sauce; and prime rib. Wines were suggested for each entree. And the price? Half as much as you'd pay in a large city. Our selections were exquisitely prepared and served without pretension. Our first thought was to applaud; our second was to move in to the Haskell House for good. The only drawback was the long drive home, but we passed the time thinking that it doesn't get any better than Jeanne's at the Haskell House in Wakefield.

Riley's
Wayne

113 S. Main St.
402-375-4345

Historically, Nebraskans haven't been picky about eating. We'll eat nearly anything and chow down nearly anywhere. We've eaten with gusto around campfires, gulped our food inside sodhouses, and tied on the feedbag in raucous saloons and frontier boardinghouses. Things haven't changed much. We'll still eat anyplace we can—converted livery stables, banks, department stores, service stations, mortuaries, and in the case of Riley's in Wayne, lumberyards. Riley's resides in a metal building that used to be a lumberyard. Inside, the food is a lot more interesting than gnawing on a two-by-four. The ambience is pleasant, with lots of green, a balcony, umbrellas at some tables, and cozy booths. The varied menu serves exotic-for-Nebraska specialties, including a very good Cajun steak soup. Forget about the fact that this was a lumberyard; it beats getting gas at a converted service station.

Sportsman's Steakhouse and Lounge
Wynot

402-357-9997

The Sportsman's Steakhouse offers a great view of the Missouri River—if you can find it. Driving there is one of the prettiest journeys in the state and, perhaps, one of the most frustrating. Tom Allen warned us in an article in the *Omaha World-Herald*. He patiently explained that, although it's right on the river and easy to find by boat, getting to the Sportsman's Steakhouse by car is nearly impossible. Tom was right. It's a challenge, but worth a try. The destination is well worth the effort, and if you get there, you can feel justifiably proud, just like an early explorer.

Here are directions from the back of the restaurant's business card. See if they're clear to you. Find the junction of state Highways 57 and 12 just southeast of Wynot. Go one mile east. Then follow the winding gravel road five miles north to the river. (Don't be distracted by the spectacular hilly scenery.) If you get lost, call the number for help.

The restaurant is an attractive cedar structure with splendid decks for viewing the river scene. The interior includes a bar from the soda fountain of the Schulte Drug Store in Hartington. The walls are covered with photos of Missouri River boats and ferries. It's basically a river roadhouse.

The food is standard steakhouse fare: the routine includes smorgasbord on Friday nights with fish and chicken, and a Sunday morning buffet. But go for the view. And what the heck, there are worse things than getting lost in scenic Cedar County.

A Hairnet With Stars

I ate at the counter.
The waitress was wearing
a hairnet with stars,
pale blue stars
over the white clouds
of her hair, a woman
still lovely at sixty
or older, full-breasted
and proud, her hands
strong and sensual,
smoothing the apron
over her belly.
I sighed and she turned
to me smiling.
"Mustard? she asked.

—Ted Kooser

Southeast

Ulbricks - Nebraska City

Granny's Cafe

Ashland

402-944-3523

The name is enough to make you want to give it á try. We did and liked it. It's granny-style cooking in a granny-style atmosphere. The sandwiches and baked goods are tasty. Try Granny's specialty—pork tenderloin.

Peter Kiewit Lodge
Mahoney State Park

Ashland

402-944-2523

Mahoney State Park is a jewel. In summer wild flowers abound. In fall the trees along the Platte provide fall color. And year around, there are all kinds of activities available: fishing, hiking, boating, swimming, trail rides, tennis, and a driving range. You can stay in the cabins sprinkled throughout the 574 acres or at Peter Kiewit Lodge. The lodge reminds us of mountain hotels with high ceilings and lots of natural wood. Many people use the facility for meetings. It serves that purpose very well, and the sleeping rooms upstairs are appealing to visitors who want a beautiful setting. A large dining room on the lower floor serves visitors and guests with daily specials and a luncheon buffet. There are evening meals, too. When we tried it, the buffet was bargain-priced at under five dollars for adults and three dollars for kids. Don't expect outstanding food, but the view of the Platte River valley is one of the best in the state.

Black Crow

Beatrice

405 Court Street
402-228-7200

We love sharing discoveries like the Black Crow in Beatrice. We want this bistro to thrive and stay in business forever.

We want to eat here when we're seventy-five, listening to Frank Sinatra and Tony Bennett, dining on the freshest ingredients, prepared as well as anywhere in the country. We want you to enjoy it, too. Just don't tell anyone else or it will be so crowded, we'll have to wait months for a table.

It is a pleasure to welcome this fine restaurant to southeast Nebraska. The Black Crow is the brainchild of talented restaurateurs, Kate Ratigan and Ray Arter. In a long, narrow storefront on Court Street, this couple has created the bistro of their dreams. Professionals who take the business seriously, they are committed to creating a pleasurable and memorable dining experience. And they succeed. The Black Crow is theater for this couple, and they want you to catch the excitement.

First of all, Kate will greet you and find you the perfect spot for the evening. Ray will be busy in the kitchen. He prepares the freshest ingredients for a menu that changes with the seasons. You'll find wonderful combinations using locally grown herbs. They're proud of roasted quail, a honey-orange glazed duckling, Cornish game hen, and fresh seafood. Pasta dishes and gourmet pizzas are delicious. Beef eaters will find a luscious choice filet. Thursday nights are ethnic nights with special offerings of creative cuisine along with the regular menu.

The servers are dressed like city waiters in blacks and whites. The white tablecloths and napkins are heavily starched. Patrons can dress casually, however, and the restaurant is not stuffy. It's a sophisticated, casual atmosphere where you are made to feel special. The lights are low, the music mellow. There's a wide variety of wines and beers.

Ask to see the scrapbook showing the before-and-after photos of the renovation. The Black Crow was salvaged after long years of hard use. The tin ceiling is original, as is the great oak back bar. It's a tasteful, classic restoration with exposed brick walls that honor the building's age.

We have enjoyed many wonderful meals here. From starters to desserts, you can't go wrong with any choice. Ray trained in both Philadelphia and France, so be prepared for first class offerings.

Impeccable service, exquisite meals, and genuine hospitality at midwestern prices draw crowds from miles around. You'd better check out the high flying Black Crow.

Mamasita's
Bennet

402-782-3000

Mamasita's. It means little mother. The name is the key to the restaurant's consistent success. Co-owner Dennis Gardner's mother is Hispanic, and she's a great cook. Fortunately she shares her cooking talent with folks throughout southeast Nebraska. She comes into Mamasita's every morning to prepare some of the Mexican dishes, and the customers obviously love her cooking.

Tim Phillips, a lawyer friend, advocates for the chile relleno. Owner Lisa Gardner says pork fajitas are a favorite. We prefer the burrito and the chicken enchilada. Probably the most sophisticated item on the menu is pollo con mole. It's chicken simmered in a spicy, dark brown sauce tasting of peanuts, chocolate, and chile. If you want a bold-tasting appetizer, try the ah chi wa wa—jalapeno peppers filled with cream cheese, deep fried, and served with a dip.

This laundromat-turned-restaurant, with its striking pink exterior, seats only about forty so most weekend evenings you have to wait to get in. If the weather is agreeable, the wait is not a problem. One evening our group sat on the front patio sipping great margaritas (regular, strawberry and raspberry) listening intently to the chimes of history from the Arp Clock and Wood Shop across the street. The chimes are recordings of classic public clocks from around the world. That night Big Ben entertained. We had a jolly good time passing the night away.

Need a fix of enchiladas, nachos or tacos? Get out of town! Head to Mamasita's in Bennet.

Anna's Restaurant   *402-234-2662*
Cedar Creek

Anna's in Cedar Creek, a tiny town halfway between Lincoln and Omaha, can't decide if it's a schoolhouse or a pub in a seaside village. This restaurant offers exquisite surroundings in rooms that resemble historic structures. Diners simply take their pick when they visit this charming restaurant with the split personality.

There is rationale for the offbeat decor. A restaurant known as the Anchor Inn existed on this spot for years. The seafaring side of Anna's pays homage to it. The schoolhouse replicates a one-room school that was moved into Cedar Creek nearly one hundred years ago. Through the years the school was transformed from its original use to become the Anchor Inn in its final metamorphosis. So while you may think the buildings are historic, they are, in fact, replicas, but very, very fine, just the same. Out back is a lighthouse and a spot for outdoor dining.

We like the schoolhouse best. It seems less a tavern than a charming restaurant, and we appreciate the fact that there is no smoking on this side. You'll really feel you're in an old schoolroom. The menus are old McGuffey readers, for example. The flag, presidential portraits, and the black, cursive handwriting charts are familiar to anyone beyond a certain age.

On the other side of the house is the pub known as the Captain's Quarters. Wood paneling, nautical artifacts, and the prow of a sailing ship are unmistakable. It's a handsome space, carefully recreated by knowledgeable craftspeople.

The meals are sophisticated and well prepared. There are chef's specials and a wide variety of big-city fare, including lobster and pheasant. Although located in a small town, the restaurant offers a menu that reflects city prices. This place gets busy; be sure to make reservations. You should also expect a wait. We've found that although everyone is very accommodating, the service is not as well organized as the rest of the restaurant. But you can while away the time looking at interesting historical artifacts.

Magic Wok
Crete

1302 Linden Ave.
402-826-5161

It doesn't matter that the Magic Wok is a fast-food restaurant located in a small town known more for kolaches than Korean pork. Nor does it matter that its location in a former Goodrich Dairy store is so Spartan that the main attraction is the huge wok where the strong-armed Korean cook stirs mounds of rice. What does matter is that for diners dismayed by the oily fare served at many fast-food oriental restaurants, the Chinese-Korean food at the Magic Wok is a reminder of how good Asian food can be.

When we first tried the Magic Wok, we couldn't believe how good it was. After all this was fast food. (Place your order at the counter. The food is served on paper plates with plastic forks.) But it's not far from our home so we've tried it again and again. Probably twenty visits. We've found the Wok consistently good.

Owned and operated by the Korean family of Jung Chun Chu, the Wok serves traditional oriental food with an emphasis on Korean specialties of the family. We sometimes start with hot and sour soup; it's tangy with sesame oil flavoring. Then we might move to Magic Wok chicken. The plate is piled high with crusty bites of chicken covered with a sweet and sour (more sour than sweet), vinegary sauce with just enough fire to make the taste buds tingle.

The Korean specialties are jam bong, a meal-in-itself soup with lots of veggies, pork, beef, shrimp and Canton noodles, plus enough heat to make your head sweat. The hot Korean pork, a family specialty, is also good. It has a slightly sweet, peppery taste. For the more traditional, there are the usual Chinese dishes, including pan-fried noodles and triple delight.

The Magic Wok is proof that fast food in a small town can be unique and delicious; so delicious that the food is equal to most of the fancier Asian restaurants in Lincoln and Omaha.

Cy's   402-566-2515
Dwight

Cy's, a forty-year fixture in Dwight, burned down in March of 1993. The folks in Dwight mourned. "This place was dead after Cy's burned down," they declared. "I don't go to the bar anymore, and, without the coffee shop, I didn't have any place to meet friends and talk." Cy's widow, Evelyn Nemec, daughter Janet, son Carl, and dozens of Dwight residents, have rebuilt Cy's, restoring the heart of the town. The rebuilt brick and clapboard cafe on the main drag is so clean you could eat off the counters.

The luncheon specials are tasty, and it makes a great excursion on Sunday morning. That's when they serve homemade donuts. Whether you're going biking on the new Oak Creek Trail that runs from Valparaiso to Brainard, or just taking a drive through the Bohemian Alps, a stop at Cy's for coffee and donuts is a treat.

Merle's Food and Drink   *402-474-6435*
Emerald

The roadhouse closest to Lincoln, Merle's attracts a sporting crowd of boaters and anglers who frequent the Salt Valley lakes. This is a casual bar and dining room with trophy animal and fish decor mounted among the beer signs. Kids will get a thrill from the huge grizzly bear in its glass case. It's also a good place to stop on football Saturdays if you're heading into Lincoln from the west. What we like best about Merle's are its efficient servers. They smile and joke, wanting to know if you want big food tonight. They know how to get the food out fast and keep you happy in the meantime. Soon you'll feel like a regular. There's sandwich fare, occasional specials, and great steaks, including a tasty one known as the Merle's special. The prime rib is also fine eating. This spot in Emerald has been a tavern for years, dating back to Lincoln's blue laws when the drinking crowd needed to get out of town to enjoy themselves. Now it's a nice destination for people who want small-town atmosphere close to the city.

Sale Barn Cafe   *402-729-3341*
The Stable   *402-729-2002*
Griffey's   *402-729-9951*
Fairbury

Sale Barn Cafe: Fairbury has several unique dining establishments that slide from one end to the other on the evolutionary scale of eateries. Starting a little lower on the scale we begin with the Sale Barn Cafe. If bovine opera is what you want, this place has it all. The meals are dirt cheap; the most expensive item on the menu is the six-ounce sirloin for $4.50. You can get fresh-baked pie and real mashed potatoes. If you don't get there before noon, you stand in line.

The Stable: Following the livestock theme, we move on to The Stable. Imagine eating with Mr. Ed; the stalls have been transformed to dining tables. Tack and beer signs are the main decor. Kim Novak, no doubt a horse lover, ate there once. Great fried chicken, charburgers, and buffalo burgers.

Griffey's: Compared to the Sale Barn and The Stable, Griffey's is downright elegant. This is a dependable restaurant serving Fairbury well. Open seven days a week from early morning until everyone goes home at night, it offers breakfast, lunch, and dinner. They have evening specials like prime rib on Saturdays and premium beverages. We prefer the back room.

Kup 'n Kettle   *604 1st St.*
Milford   *402-761-2442*

We used to have a Saturday morning ritual. We'd hop in the car and drive eight miles cross-country to Milford, home of the Kup 'n Kettle. We tried to get there early enough to beat the locals to the freshly baked rolls and donuts.

Then disaster struck. The Kup 'n Kettle closed. What to do? Where to go on Saturday mornings for coffee, breakfast, and a final donut for the road? Withdrawal pangs lasted two years. Just as we were getting used to deprivation, something wonderful happened. The Kup re-opened.

Although reborn as a Daylight Donut franchise, nothing has changed. Whatever the reincarnation, we still call it the Kup 'n Kettle. And the name still adorns the building which is next door to the post office on Milford's wide main drag. If you get there after 9 a.m., don't linger by the front door— you'll be trampled by a stampede of hungry Milfordites looking for their Saturday morning fix. If you dally till 9:30, you may have to wait for a table or stand while you devour a pecan roll.

They still serve scrumptious, home-style breakfasts. Omelettes and biscuits and gravy—oh my! Pancakes and hash browns and sausage--to die! Lunches also draw a crowd with midwestern cafe fare bound to give you plenty of energy for hauling hay, hoeing the garden, or taking a nap. Yes, the Kup 'n Kettle and Saturday mornings have been revived.

Lied Conference Center   *402-873-8733*
Nebraska City

Located at the Arbor Day Farm near Arbor Lodge in the Arbor Day city, the Lied Conference Center's emphasis is on trees. The center is built of huge, Douglas fir logs from Oregon, and it has the ambience of an elegant hunting lodge. It's a great place for conferences or family vacations. Visitors can swim in the indoor pool, work out in the fitness center, and hike or jog on beautiful trails around the grounds. The dining room features views across apple orchards to the Morton mansion, known as Arbor Lodge, the home of the founder of Arbor Day. The dining room has resolved some of its early problems and the food is good. The luncheon buffets are guaranteed to bring on the need to—perish the thought— saw logs.

Teresa's Family Restaurant
Nebraska City

812 Central Ave.
402-873-9100

We first heard about Teresa's pies in a feature article in *The New York Times*. The author raved about them during a weeklong visit to the area. Seems like she ate a pie a day for a week. Teresa's could make you do that. The pies are good to the last crumb. The luncheon specials, regular hometown vittles, lean toward meat-and-potato classics.

Ulbrick's
Nebraska City

1513 So. 11th
402-873-5458

Any trencherman worthy of the name will have found his way to Ulbrick's by now. The appetite-impaired should steer clear of this place; don't you dare go near it. Ulbrick's is the ultimate for the plain-food, hearty-eater crowd. If that describes you, get in the car today and drive to Ulbrick's in Nebraska City.

This Highway 75 roadhouse is located in a converted gas station. We'll pass on the chance for a pun. Like a gas station, its decor is utilitarian. Chrome, vinyl, and plastic create a no-nonsense air, as if reminding you that your business here is to eat. Nothing fancy about the servers either. They're usually local teenagers, eclectic in their jeans, T-shirts, and Nikes, on a mission to keep the food coming as fast as possible.

This is big food. Some of the largest human beings in the Midwest happily tie into the family-style fare at Ulbrick's. And they always look happy.

Among old-timers, this famous eatery is known as Mary's, which separates the initiated from the ignorant. Founded by Mary Ulbrick in 1944, it hasn't missed a beat under the direction of Mary's daughter, Charlene Chapin. Charlene follows her mother's success formula. The star of the menu is fried chicken, cooked the old-fashioned way in a cast-iron skillet, crusty and delicious. She also offers steaks, ham, and shrimp. Side dishes provide an impressive support team. There are three salads for starters: lettuce, spicy sauerkraut slaw, and a tapioca-marshmallow-citrus whip we used to call ambrosia. What a combination! In addition, there's creamed corn, creamed cabbage, green beans, potatoes, homemade noodles, rolls, and dessert. Where in the world is a trencherman going to find this kind of variety and volume? And they fill up the side dishes any time you ask for more.

We also recommend the pies and Mary's cookbook. It contains her cooking secrets, pictures of her grandchildren, and such helpful hints as carrots peeled under warm water will not leave a stain on the hands.

When you waddle out, you, too, will have a smile on your face and the satisfied look of an experienced trencherman. Then start calling the place Mary's and act like you knew about it all along.

Hallie's
Pawnee City

604 9th St.
402-852-2445

Hallie's restaurant in Pawnee City is proof that sisters can work together to accomplish good things. From a family dream, Hallie's was born. This was not a simple process by any means. Hallie's is a restored stately home. The Klepper sisters, Annette Hinrichsen, Becki Smith and Jenett Reed, with the help of their husbands, brought the Hallie Henry house back to life after years of neglect. It's now a pretty treasure sitting on the east side of Highway 50.

Enjoy made-from-scratch luncheon and dinner fare on the first floor. Upstairs are gift boutiques and an art gallery honoring the Klepper matriarch. This is a lovely setting for a nice meal.

Keller's II   402-795-2544
Pleasant Dale

We can't imagine Pleasant Dale without Ila and Harry Keller. They've been serving good food for years now, and as their name implies, this is their second go around as Pleasant Dale cafe owners. To open Keller's II, they put up a new building, which includes a game room, dining room, bar, and a meeting room in the basement. Plus, they built the first skybox in the state with a screened-in porch overlooking the Pleasant Dale ball diamond. There's one special feature in the decor. You shouldn't miss the whimsical mounted steer surrounded by a hand-painted trompe l'oeil barn scene. The steer wears seasonal hats just to keep things lively.

Serving breakfast, lunch and dinner seven days a week, the cafe is a draw for lots of people in the area. They have typical bar food plus cafe specials that attract a regular crowd. For people who prefer a cafe atmosphere to a dark bar or tavern, this is an attractive alternative. The friendly servers, Jenny, Loree, and Debbie, know nearly everyone. Cook John Harry loves to make pies. You might find six varieties plus apple cake with caramel sauce on any given night. Delicious homemade soups are always served, and there are specials at noon and at night. Sunday noons are busy. So are Tuesday nights when the special is a pan-fried chicken dinner. Only one hundred chickens are served so it's important to get there early—the patrons truly flock in.

PD Quick Shop
Pleasant Dale

402-795-3663

We admit this is a strange pick, but the PD Quick Stop, a convenience store owned by the local co-op, has a couple of items that are more than just convenient. Go early for the kolaches. Rumor has it that they're some of the best you can find in southeast Nebraska. (Sorry, Wilber.) Folks drive out of their way to buy a dozen or so. You can, too. If you call in the night before, the morning baker will make them special at 4:30 a.m. Otherwise, you take what you get. You might also want to sample the pies and pick up some Fairbury hot dogs.

Porky's
Pleasant Dale

402-795-9915

Porky's in Pleasant Dale, located in an old bank building, is the only spot of architectural interest in this little town. The old building, painted a brick red with a mural on its south side, has been a cafe and beer hall for years. Look for the egg-carton ceiling, an early version of acoustical tile. Given its tiny kitchen, grill food is featured, but the bar has a regular clientele who like to spend time with Porky on the weekends and play keno. He does the typical Friday fish fry and giant steaks on Sundays. Saturday is prime rib night. Porky is a promoter: he held the first ostrich feed in the state. The town ball diamond is right out his back door and he brings in national bands for outdoor concerts a couple of times a year. If you don't want to fight the crowds in Seward, try the Pleasant Dale Fourth of July celebration. It's a little smaller scale, but you can enjoy the show with a brew at Porky's.

Camp Rulo
Rulo

An English proverb says that fish must swim three times—
once in the water, a second time in the sauce, and a third
time in wine in the stomach. That's kind of the way it goes
at Camp Rulo. The carp and catfish are caught fresh each
day in the Missouri River that runs alongside the restaurant. Coated in a light batter and fried to a golden brown, the
fish may not be swimming in sauce, but they can be drenched
in lemon and tartar sauce if that's the way you like them.
Cold beer is the best accompaniment to these tender morsels.

Camp Rulo has followed a successful formula for years and
years. When the original building burned, a new, spiffed-up
Camp Rulo was rebuilt on the banks of the Big Mo. Nostalgic
diners will miss the dumpy, backwoods look. What hasn't
changed, however, is the mesmerizing view from the big
windows. Enjoy some of the Midwest's finest, freshest fried
fish as you watch the Missouri River's slow drift to the Gulf
of Mexico. You won't even have to fib about the big ones that
got away.

Peppercorn
Seward

South Hwy. 15
402-643-9090

Restaurants in Seward suffer a bit because of the community's
proximity to Lincoln. Local residents who want fine dining
often drive to Lincoln. Until recently, if you didn't want to
eat fast food or go to a tavern, you were out of luck.

A relative newcomer to town, the Peppercorn is quickly
becoming a local leader. Located on Highway 15 just south
of Seward, this restaurant/sports bar has been recognized as

the best eatery in town. A wide selection of menu items, well-organized staff, and a sports motif make this a good reason to pull off I-80. It's also a draw for college students at Concordia College or Southeast Community College in Milford.

Lincoln residents ought to take the scenic drive west on Highway 34, explore Seward's pretty town square and the neighborhoods around Concordia College, and then head south on 15 for a bite to eat at the Peppercorn. Avoid the fast-food outlets on the south Seward strip and give this fine place a try.

Springfield Drug
Springfield

205 Main St.
402-253-2000

The feature here is the old-fashioned soda fountain with museum-quality drugstore antiques. There are the familiar, lovable malts, splits, sundaes, chocolate cokes, phosphates, and Green Rivers.

Salty Dog
Steele City

402-442-2233

The Salty Dog is a fun-loving, raucous place. It may be a little rough around the edges, but it bears mention because Steele City is a good town to visit, and the bar is peopled with colorful characters. We've seen renegades from the sixties, bikers, farmers, locals, and wide-eyed strangers huddled over brews in this beer hall. The jukebox plays classics to eat burgers and drink beer by. There are crazy juxtapositions. On the wall a sign says I Brake For Hallucinations. On the antique floor are old octagonal floor tiles with a four-color border and a snowflake design.

Mexican food is the strength of the menu. Everything is called super. There are super tacos, super enchiladas, and a super-duper burrito—a flour tortilla stuffed with meat, beans, cheese, black olives, and onions drenched in sauce with a side salad. We loved the dog wings—a Salty Dog version of buffalo wings swimming in a pool of special blue cheese sauce and dill spears.

Co-owner Margo D'Angelo says, "We don't claim to be a five-star restaurant and neither are the prices, but the food, I'm sure, can compete! The hungriest of the litter is always satisfied. The Salty Dog has always been a gathering place for flamboyant, colorful, crazy characters. We sometimes get a few hound dogs who enjoy howling at the moon. Please feel free to join in."

Instead of howling in the tavern, take a look at the rest of the town. There's an intriguing, old livery stable and a bank building and Baptist church built in the early 1880s. These charming buildings cry out for restoration. We can envision a colorful artists' colony in Steele City. It has nearly all the basics now—outrageous characters and a reliable watering hole in the Salty Dog.

The Old Cafe
Tecumseh

On the Square
402-335-3457

An old, southeast Nebraska favorite, Helen's Cafe, has re-emerged from a fire with a face-lift, a new name, and a new owner, Janet Young. But she wants everyone to know that the good old days are back by calling her enterprise the Old Cafe. Mrs. Young comes from an old-time Tecumseh family, and she's proud to bring this place back into operation. Surprisingly, Mrs. Young was a schoolmate of Helen, the original proprietor of this homey cafe, and Helen's been known to drop in now and then to give tips to the new management.

This cafe has been prettified. There are new tan booths, a chair rail border of cute wallpaper, and the family collection of old plates and cuckoo clocks arranged around the room. There's not a hint of its former lives as a Masonic Hall and post office.

The 1880s building, on the National Register of Historic Places, is but one attractive element in what may be one of Nebraska's most picturesque town squares. It's easy to see why it was chosen for the filming of the TV miniseries "Amerika." The centerpiece of the square is the 1888 court-house designed in a form inspired by the U.S. Capitol.

From 6:00 a.m. to 8:00 p.m., this is a family place where you can stoke up on a big breakfast of ham and eggs or pancakes and enjoy hot roast beef sandwiches for lunch (or dinner as its known is rural Nebraska) and filling suppers for the whole family. In the center is a round table for the town regulars who help themselves to coffee by the honor system. Keeping things running are Mrs. Young's son and daughter-in-law, Robert and Lori, who've done most of the reconstruc-tion themselves.

The Old Cafe is the very essence of a small-town life. It's where people stop in for coffee, visit about crops and the weather, complain about politics, and discuss Friday night's game. But the function of cafes like this goes beyond social. It's the town communication center, the first place to learn about news. It's rural CNN. As a local cafe fan told us, "I go to our cafe to find out what the heck's going on around here."

Memo to Marge

Let me tell you nothing's pithier
than the one-fingered wave.

The exclamation point which splits
a farmer's smile,

it's the national flag of Nebraska,
and our haiku of the plains.

I've seen waving with a single finger
extend the cabs of pickups,

supercharge combines
while filling every ditch with sun.

And on minimum maintenance roads
the damned thing's

a blunt-fingered wand
the world's most efficient halloo.

working only as hard as it has to

—Don Welch

North Central

Robert Hanna

Double T Cafe & Lounge
Halsey, Nebraska

Our Place
Ainsworth

East Hwy. 20
402-387-0690

Hazel Platt and John Stec, new owners of Our Place (formerly the Golden Steer), have a surprise for you. The outside of Our Place is rather plain, but inside there's an ornate garden gate, bubbling fountain, sculpture, deep carpeting, and luxurious decorations. What's more, the decorations change with the seasons. Hazel Platt obviously likes to decorate, and fortunately, she also likes food. She started as a waitress after high school and has been in the business ever since. Her partner, John Stec, has sixteen years of restaurant experience.

The food complements the decor. Although steak is big, they have a nice variety of seafood: Mediterranean shrimp, walleye, halibut, catfish, and rainbow trout. There are daily dinner specials. Be sure to try the homemade onion rings. Our Place is a pleasant surprise.

Smet's Cafe
Anselmo

308-749-2226

The restaurant business is survival of the fittest. Most start-ups last about a year. But we've found a survivor; veteran of fifty years in the restaurant wars, Howard Smet returned from the service in 1946 and on April Fools' Day the same year, opened his cafe. It's been going strong ever since.

What's the formula for success? In addition to lots of hard work and stamina, the Smets have another ingredient. In the summer they feature fresh vegetables from their nearby garden. Howard and wife Lucille grow and serve every kind of vegetable—cabbage, tomatoes, broccoli, corn. One after-noon when we called, Howard was snapping beans. In the winter the canned goods show up in homemade soups, like potato and vegetable.

Obviously, vegetables are not the only reason for their success. They know how to cook. Howard was trained in the army so he does most of the cooking. It's solid, sleeves-up food, like ham and baked steak. Lucille makes the pies. Her specialties are cherry, sour cream, and a mincemeat, made from scratch. And get this, Howard and Lucille, both in their 80s, have no plans for retirement. Obviously their cooking is not only good for business; it's good for their health.

The main dining room of the cafe is the former bank build-ing. Later the Smets bought the building next door and made it another dining room. Someone drove through the plate-glass window, lowering the storage value of the building and the selling price as well. That's when the Smets bought it. No wonder they're survivors.

Howard says there's one disadvantage to being successful for so long: underpriced promotions come back from the past to haunt you. A New York visitor dropped in the other day with a card that said Good For One Free Cup Of Coffee At Smets Cafe, Anselmo, Nebraska. Howard gave away those cards ten years ago!

Range Cafe
Bassett

402-684-3379

Bassett is where ranch country begins. Local ranchers decided they needed a hotel to put up their cattle customers, so they built one. But more important than a hotel, they needed a restaurant for those customers and for themselves, so they built one—the Range Cafe. The Range Cafe special-izes in beef, naturally, and it has to please the toughest customer of all, the producer. At the Range Cafe the atmo-sphere is western, the cowboys and ranchers are abundant, and the steaks are world class.

Golden Nugget   308-996-9260
Boelus

The sign on the edge of town says Home of Famous Ball Teams and the Golden Nugget Visited by Famous People. The famous people are local celebrity Roger Welsch and CBS television anchor Charles Kuralt, who stopped in at the Nugget when doing his *On the Road* series.

Located four miles south of Nysted, about three miles north of St. Michael, and ten miles southwest of Rockville, Boelus is not, in any sense of the word, in the thick of things. It's clear that the Nugget's success through the years is due to good food—a lot of good food—at very reasonable prices. The place has changed hands several times recently, but you can still get a good steak. In fact, one of Nebraska's lunker steaks—a twenty-two-ounce T-Bone—is found at the Nug-get. And if you ask, locals still enjoy telling about the time Kuralt's crew spent a Saturday evening there.

Uncle Buck's   308-547-2210
Brewster

From the banks of the North Loup River, we've watched this monster lodge emerge. At last we had a chance to visit this incredible place during the dinner hour, and on a weekend to boot. Uncle Buck's is a unique blend of cowboy steakhouse and elegant western inn. Groups can rent rooms for meetings or reunions and gather in an impressive, two-story great room filled with trophy animals and steer heads, cowhides draped over balconies, and western art on the walls. The only thing lacking is a massive, stone fireplace. You must see this space to believe it. During hunting season, it must be jam-packed.

The heart of the lodge is a saloon and dining room built in rugged, contemporary western style—lots of rough wood on the walls, bare wood floors laid on the diagonal, and western artifacts. Its distinctive atmosphere would be out of place anywhere else in the state.

The food seemed ordinary with typical steaks and sandwiches, but homemade white and wheat rolls showed a deft touch. Maybe we had an off-night for some reason. The salad bar with specialty salads reminiscent of covered dish suppers also showed promise.

The atmosphere is casual to say the least. Little kids and toddlers careened through the restaurant on big wheels and pedal toys, motoring back and forth between a poolroom and the great room where their families dined in peace. Nobody seemed to mind. At the next table, a group of seven ranchers and cowboys was talking about an upcoming roping. A lively group, hosted by the Wieses of North Platte and Thedford, was at the next table. Judy Wiese visited with nearly everyone who looked like a stranger, and she made us feel welcome to the neighborhood.

This enterprise is the brainchild of a local ranch family who want to try their hands at being innkeepers and restaurateurs. We didn't get a chance to check the sleeping rooms, but if they match the rest of the place, they're comfortable indeed. When locals and visitors want to honky-tonk, there's a bar and dance hall in the walkout basement. Those who imbibe a bit too much can simply stroll upstairs to find a spot to sleep it off. This place could catch on. Get there soon to enjoy the Sandhills hospitality.

Charlene's
Broken Bow

308-872-3340

Bill Erickson, one of Broken Bow's leading citizens, recommended Charlene's. We were suspicious about his advice because the restaurant is just across the street from his law office. He protested that he would "guarantee the meat loaf and strawberry pie are world class. Trust me." We worry when a lawyer's best argument is "trust me." We tried the meat loaf and a smothered hamburger with carrots, potatoes, and salad bar for the price of only $4.95 each. We concur with counsel that Charlene's cooking is good and bet he'd be willing to walk a lot farther to eat at Charlene's.

Lobby Restaurant
Broken Bow

308-872-3363

In the Lobby Restaurant, hotel doors with room numbers intact cleverly define the boundaries of each cafe booth, a nod to the restaurant's home, the Arrow Hotel in Broken Bow. The food varies in quality, but this middle-of-cow-country restaurant may have found a good hand in Harold Patsios. He's been there since late 1993, and the quality and variety of food are more consistent.

Harold reports an unusual guest joins the breakfast bunch on occasion, although it isn't one of the regulars. Harold walked outside one morning and startled a deer on the sidewalk. The deer jumped through the hotel's plate-glass window. Smelling pancakes, it wandered through the hotel lobby and into the restaurant. It pranced around tables, sniffed the omelette of a terrified diner, and found its way out without leaving a tip.

The standard cafe fare, including good Nebraska steaks, is offered, and the prime rib is hand-rubbed with special seasonings and cooked to juicy perfection. A Greek salad and gyro sandwich are among the more unusual items. At lunch you'll typically find open-faced hot sandwiches (turkey, ground beef, and beef) and a full salad bar. There's also a popular Sunday buffet.

Tony's Restaurant
308-485-4664

Cairo

When three enthusiastic, oversized eaters recommend a restaurant, we listen. Tim Mohanna, one of the owners of the Record Printing Company in Cairo and printer of this book, is the largest printer in Nebraska—he's six feet ten inches tall. Obviously Tim has to do a lot of eating, and he recommends Tony's Restaurant in Cairo. Roger Welsch, premier Nebraska humorist from nearby Dannebrog and a legendary trencherman, wrote us touting Tony's. Noted Lincoln trial lawyer Rod Rehm, a husky barrister, lauds Tony's as "great home-cooked food with a Greek owner who features Greek dishes." He had the marinated chicken and proclaimed it "well worth the money and the drive out from Grand Island." With recommendations like that, we had to check it out.

Tony's is one of the first roadhouses as you travel west on Nebraska's scenic Highway 2. And it may be the only Greek roadhouse in the state. Owner Sophia Jantzi says "My sister (Christina Tzirikidis) and I are Greek and we are 'great cooks' and we put a little bit of Greece or 'grease' into everything we do." Nothing like a cook who throws a little humor into the mixing bowl! When asked the main reason for her success, Sophia replied tongue in cheek, "our personalities, our bubbly charm, our recipes." Meeting this lady is worth the trip.

The sisters' specialties are cabbage rolls, marinated chicken, Greek bread, Greek salads, and gyro sandwiches. The gyros are shaved layers of spicy beef topped with onions, sour cream, and tomatoes in a homemade pita. Call and find out when they're serving their "once-a-month Greek special," an eating orgy worthy of a marathon run from almost anywhere in the state.

Here's what food enthusiast Roger Welsch wrote about Tony's.

"Most of the food is just good ol' small-town fare—but aha! Sophie is terminally Greek. So skip the roast beef and hamburgers and tie into one of her gyros. Or two. *Incredible!* The pita bread is homemade and absolutely ambrosial. If she has baklava, of course, eat baklava, but otherwise her pie a la mode is superior."

Roger closed his letter to us with a kind offer: "If you ever need something eaten, be sure to let me know. I'm good at it. I do it all the time. A lot."

With recommendations like these from Roger, Rod, and Tim, world-class eaters, what more can we say? Eat at Tony's—soon.

Danish Baker

Dannebrog

The *Grand Island Independent* dubbed Tom Schroeder the "philosopher king of Dannebrog's cafe society." Tom Schroeder is even more than that; he's a classic small-town hero: friendly, devout, generous, and gregarious. He's known for his quick wit and gentle philosophical observations. We call them Schroederisms.

In 1991 Tom opened the Danish Baker, a combination bakery, card parlor, social hall, and cafe. In the morning customers chat, play cards, drink coffee, and help themselves to Tom's baked goods, fresh from the previous day. Tom's a novel baker. "I don't get up at 4 a.m!" he reports. "If you want fresh-baked goods, come in the afternoon." Tom bakes bread, kolaches, rolls, and his specialty cookies, from chocolate chip to molasses.

Lunches are "what I feel like fixing." He offers a special each day: might be chicken and noodles over mashed potatoes, macaroni and cheese with sausage on the side, or ham and scalloped potatoes. That's it for the day. No menu. All you can eat for $2.50.

Although he believes in keeping it simple at noon, Tom loves to stage special events. On Thursday nights he woos his crowd with homemade pizza: medium crust, crisp on the outside and doughy on the inside. The sauce is understated and delicate because "it's not supposed to overpower everything else." Next comes cheese and a variety of toppings. One Thursday evening he served 114 pies. At noon on the third Saturday, it's potluck. Everyone brings something and Tom provides coffee, rolls, and dessert.

Tom's cooking style has evolved from childhood. "My mother always wanted me to taste what she was cooking. I learned how things should taste. And that's why I'm a good cook." Regarding small towns, he laughs: "People in small towns know everything you do before you even do it. When you make a mistake, you might as well come back and just tell everyone about it." One of his heroes is wife, Carol: "Honest, hardworking, and she loves me—that says a lot. She's the best person I've ever met." He believes you should "never do anything just for the money" and knows there "isn't anyone in the world who isn't worth talking to."

He prizes relationships in Dannebrog. "We interact. People care about you." His goodwill extends to his competition down the street, Harriett's Danish. He couldn't say enough fine things about Harriett and her cooking. And about Roger Welsch he said, "He put Dannebrog on the map. He has shown the world what small-town life is like."

A visit to the Danish Baker will fill you with good food, good company, good feelings, and if you listen carefully, Tom Schroeder's good philosophy.

Harriett's Danish   *308-226-2322*
Dannebrog

If someone asked the best indicator of a good restaurant, we'd say it's a place where the owner **is** the restaurant. Good restaurant owners are a constant presence in their establishments; they love people and like to be out amongst them, pressing the flesh like good politicians. They crave pleasing people, and they ought to know a thing or two about good service and good food. Harriett's Danish in Dannebrog fits this formula. Harriett Nielsen **is** Harriett's Danish. She's owner, manager, hostess, sometime waitress, and most importantly, the main cook. People say visiting her restaurant is like going to your Danish grandma's house, an apt description.

For our first visit, Art and Rosemary accompanied us on a Sunday morning. Art, who really had a Danish grandmother, wanted to try the special smorgasbord. Driving into town, we couldn't miss Harriett's. Red and white Danish flags marked the entrance, and the sign said Harriett's Speise Hus.

We passed through a doorway into the kitchen to pick up our plates and silverware among the folks doing the cooking. This was, after all, the Sunday buffet, and they were cooking for a crowd. Diners gathered in four small rooms adjoining the kitchen. The walls were decorated with Harriett's collection of blue Danish Christmas plates, Scandinavian wall hangings, and American antiques. There was also a bound collection of the *Dannebrog Times* up to 1949.

The buffet table was heaped with Harriett's interpretation of Danish-American dishes: various kinds of salads, steaming bowls of vegetables, casseroles, frikedelle (meatballs), fried chicken, homemade rye bread, and a variety of delicious desserts. Art smiled. We lugged our heaping plates to a table we shared with a family that had driven 75 miles to eat at the restaurant; we'd driven even farther. We ate pounds of great food for an outlandishly low price. As we waddled out, well satisfied, Art resolved that we should never eat again.

A few weeks later, however, we gave up that resolution and came back for Harriett's only evening meal—the Thursday aebleskivers. They're round pancakes, a Danish specialty, made in a unique cast-iron pan. They're a little larger than golf balls, and as you can imagine, go down much easier. Golden brown and crispy, they're sublime covered with powdered sugar and drenched in maple syrup. Early birds will be pleased that Harriett also serves breakfast. Order pancakes. Roger Welsch describes them as incredible and swears they're so thin they have only one side. Order eggs (they're from Roger's chickens) and diced hashbrowns (if you try them first, Roger's eggs will get cold before you get to them).

We'll always be grateful to Art for steering us to this first-rate cafe, and thankful to Harriett for her tender attention to details.

Nila's   *308-863-2314*
Elba

Seems like some local folks in Dannebrog want to escape their little town when the out-of-towners flock to Harriett's big Sunday buffet. Well-fed foodies flee to Nila's in Elba for cooking that, in their opinion, ranks right up there with Harriett's. Now that's a good recommendation! Located in a bank building, the eatery features Sunday buffets that are the big draw. They'll remind you of the best potluck you've every had. Call ahead, they're *not* held every week.

The Country Neighbor   *308-346-5049*
Elyria

Restoration is rampant in Loup County. Fort Hartsuff, an excellent example of a restored frontier fort, is a must see. Established to protect area settlers from attack, the fort saw heated battles; three medals of honor for bravery during one battle were issued to soldiers stationed there. Fort Hartsuff will take you back one hundred years.

The second restoration project, only a half mile south of the fort, is The Country Neighbor. Two local farm couples have restored and transformed an 1870s schoolhouse into a pleasant place to stop for a country breakfast, a sandwich-and-soup lunch, or refreshments of fresh-baked cookies, rolls, pie, and gourmet teas and coffees. Stop at the Neighbor for a rest; it'll restore you, too.

Hungry Horse Saloon
308-653-3100
Ericson

Some people say that you can't believe anything saloon owner Frank Wietzki says. The longtime owner of the Hungry Horse is known for his pranks. For instance, Wietzki started quite a commotion when he hung up a presidential Certificate of Award for Prime Rib—signed by George Bush. When patrons were thrilled with the award, he confessed that things got a little out of hand. "I hung it up as a joke," Frank says, "and everybody went ape over it." He also admits that "the meat is good, but maybe not that good." When we asked the most unique dish on the menu, he said lettuce soup. Frank just can't stop kidding.

Unique? The owner **and** this place are unique. In 1985 a UNL student wrote her thesis about the saloon. Called *One Horse Town*, it unravels the infamous and widespread legend of the foot stompin', whiskey-guzzling Hungry Horse Saloon. Now don't you wish you'd done that kind of research in college? On the other hand, maybe you did.

There are many stories about the Horse that aren't in the thesis. A friend who grew up in the area says he's seen cowboys on horseback inside the saloon on a Saturday night. One local hero, on a $50 bet, zipped up and down the main street in a snowmobile, buck naked. The saloon also sponsors the famous Sandhills Turtle Race in August and a non-PGA sanctioned event known as the Hungry Horse Pasture Golf Classic. In September it hosts dog races.

Frank seems to think he has to keep things lively in Ericson, and he's probably right. The business district in this town is little more than a wide spot in the road. The Hungry Horse and the sale barn are the sole enterprises.

Liveliness and authenticity count. Like most antiques, the Hungry Horse could use a bit of sprucing up, but that would ruin its patina. The place has the look of a gritty beer hall, the bar well scarred as though a thousand shots of red eye have crossed its surface. The rough paneling is decorated with local brands, and the linoleum is bruised with the scuffs of boots. The bar and the dance floor are separated by the fringe of a workhorse fly harness.

When you feel like being rowdy, throw on your boots and jeans and spend Saturday night at Nebraska's most authentic, and reportedly wildest, western saloon. And we're not kidding!

Nebraska Inn   *402-583-9922*
Gross

For several years running in this tiny town, the ratio of citizens to cafes was two to one. Gross is experiencing a population boom; the ratio is now nine to one. The one is the Nebraska Inn. Things aren't crowded in Gross. You won't be crowded at the inn unless you go on Friday or Saturday nights when the population increases by astounding proportions for the special steak dinners. On Monday, Wednesday, and Friday noon there are family-style lunches for big eaters. What's more, you'll find super burgers at all times and a cup of coffee for a nickel. Can't beat that.

Double J-T Cafe and Bar 308-458-2332
at the Hyannis Hotel
Hyannis

This is a good spot for getting up-close and personal with real cowboys. Dudes will have to take a backseat in this tiny cafe, coffee shop, and tavern because there are probably more cowfolk per square feet in this place than anywhere else in the state.

Open seven days a week, the cafe offers full meals in the evening—there's prime rib night and Mexican night, for example—and luncheon specials and breakfast items all day long. The newest owners have made remarkable progress sprucing up this old establishment. New bathrooms are a real plus, and it looks like more improvements are on the way, including renovation of some of the sleeping rooms upstairs. It's a pleasure to stop here now; the coffee pot is always on, and the conversation is always lively.

The Bakery Cafe 402-569-2646
Lynch

On Fridays look for great hot beef sandwiches at The Bakery Cafe. Every third Thursday Indian tacos draw folks from fifty miles away. Owner Carla Wilson keeps five children well fed at home, and she'll feed you well, too, with daily lunch specials. Carla's homemade rolls and pies are the only baked goods served.

Bowring Ranch State Park

Merriman

308-684-3428

Our most unusual meal was served in a sodhouse at the Bowring Ranch State Park north of Merriman. We stopped at the visitor center to learn more about the ranch, and then wandered through the barnyard where there were chickens and geese. Out on the range were a few head of cattle, descendants of the original Bowring herd. A sodhouse surrounded by flower beds, a kitchen garden, and herbs was tucked away on a corner of the property behind the fine, white, clapboard, family home. We had a wonderful surprise when we strolled to the soddy for a closer look; it was tended by a delightful woman, Ardith Morton, who calls herself the Sodhouse Lady. She encouraged us to come in to see the tiny two-room soddy and to try home-cooked pioneer fare. We certainly did not expect a delicious light repast of fried green tomatoes, bannock bread, and coffee. Everything was prepared on a massive, woodburning, cast-iron cookstove in the sodhouse by the Sodhouse Lady herself. She serves her treats while telling stories about the Bowrings and the settlement of the Sandhills.

She's not there every day, but if you call in advance, she'll fire up the stove and prepare a special treat for you to enjoy as she tells about the colorful history of the region. You can also tour the Bowring home and view exquisite collectibles acquired through the years by Mrs. Bowring, a former U.S. Senator.

The Bowring Ranch is a great stop on your Sandhills tour, and the Sodhouse Lady's meal is an unexpected accompaniment.

Naper Cafe

402-832-5272

Naper

This cafe, located in the tiny village of Naper, is owned by the village. Manager Vivian Alexander reports the secret of its success: "We're friendly and serve good food." What else is there?

The Diner

117 N. 16th St.
308-728-5856

Ord

The fun of exploring smaller towns in Nebraska is the chance for discovery. The Diner in Ord, formerly known as Douthit's Diner, was just such a chance encounter.

Driving through town, we spotted a pretty, green-striped awning, flower pots, and benches in front of a little store-front. When we stopped for a look, we discovered wonderful people working hard to create hospitality.

Mary Lister and Brandi Roger, who have eight children between them and, evidently, too much time on their hands, have recently leased this property to develop a restaurant. The Diner serves breakfast, lunch, and dinner in a charming dining room with many unusual features.

In the front room is a salad bar/breakfast bar made of old wooden fixtures from a general store. It's attractive and very convenient. As you walk to the lounge in back, you'll see picture windows looking out on a little passage cut between two buildings. Clever murals painted on the walls outside provide diners an attractive view, a whimsical touch.

We ordered the seafood platter to go and enjoyed bite-sized morsels of deep-fried shellfish and delicious catfish. We'd have to come back often to try everything this place offers. One feature, however, needs special mention. The cafe stays open on weekend evenings to offer a midnight breakfast. The bar closes at midnight to offer breakfast until 2 a.m., a great innovation for people who want to have a bite to eat and a cup of coffee before the long drive home.

This place has the right spirit—gracious hospitality, a desire to please, and a willingness to innovate to better serve customers. We wish them luck and encourage you to give them a try.

Gin's Tavern

Rockville

308-372-7275

When we walked into this tavern, we told owner, Gin, a spry fifty-something woman, that a friend had said this was the place to get good, cheap hamburgers. "Your friend's got good taste," she said, popping the tab on a can of classic Coke. "It's the best place in town." "But isn't this the only place in town?" we noted, having spied only a bank, post office, and Gin's in downtown Rockville. "Don't get picky," she replied. "How do you like your burgers?" Seems we had just missed burger nite—Fridays—when the burgers are ninety cents for a quarter-pounder.

We watched the grill as Gin fried up some juicy burgers. She slapped the buns on the grill to warm them a bit and give them the steamy, slippery feel we remember from childhood. We knew they'd be good, and they were.

We spied some homemade coconut cream pie on the cooler shelf to the left of the beer. The pie was good—just like the burger. For burgers like those from your childhood, and at almost the same price, try Gin's.

Cattleman's Restaurant and Lounge   *308-762-8347*
Seneca

Cattleman's is a new steakhouse in a once booming, now shrinking town. Cattle are the only business in Seneca. You can eat them at Cattleman's, or buy them for your kids at the Critter Corral, a manufacturer of toy horses and bulls.

Steaks taste better in cattle country. At least they taste mighty good at Cattleman's. There may be better things than a sizzling Sandhills steak—but probably not.

The Bridge Club   *308-942-9916*
Taylor

The focal point of the Bridge Club is the long, harvest-crew table that invites customers to join the group and the free-flowing discussion. The arrangement throws strangers in with the locals, who look you over like the newest gunfighter in town. But once you get past the staring stage, sit down, ask a few questions, and pretty soon you'll see they like visitors. The only duel from then on will be verbal. The chow is typical cafe; however, your friends at the long table will tell you the chicken-fried steak is the best in Nebraska. The name has nothing to do with cards—Bridge is the owner's last name.

Cowpoke Inn   *308-645-2625*
Thedford

When you ask what's for dinner in the Sandhills, there's only one answer—beef. Beef is king at the Cowpoke Inn. The cattlemen in the Sandhills are loyal to their product, and whether it's what they're eating or what they're talking about, beef is front and center at the Cowpoke Inn. Expect plenty of local color and a parade of personalities. The ranchers and cowboys at the Cowpoke munch on burgers and chew on steaks while speaking in a tongue foreign to city folk. You'll hear talk of weaning weight indexes, EPDs, calving scores, exotics, and AI. You'll also hear talk of politics occasionally and weather a lot.

Roberta Johnson, a rancher's daughter from north of Thedford, took over the spread in February, 1995. A registered nurse, she cares about her customers, and the inn shows her hospitality. The beef is good, the service friendly, and the beer is cold.

Sowders Ranch Store
Tryon

308-587-2333

We love this western version of a general store, soda fountain, saddlery, and convenience store all rolled into one. The Sowders are a ranch family who, with warmth and good spirits, offer nearly anything you need. They are promoters of the western life, publishing a little newspaper and generously passing out free coffee to anyone who stops by. Have an old-fashioned malt, their specialty. Need a hat? Buy it here. Pick up some boots, too. Need some grub? Take a look at the grocery shelves. They'll even stitch up your saddle if it's busted. If by chance you pass through Tryon, don't pass up this great stop.

Jordan's
Valentine

Highway 20
402-376-1255

On the north side of Highway 20 as it passes through Valentine, you'll find an eatery that's truly trying to cover all its bases. This plain-looking building, surrounded by gravel parking lots, is a triple threat—a sports bar/cafe/fine dining complex.

Here's how it works. You pick the right hours and approach the place from the right direction, and you'll find what you want. If you use the west door, you'll enter a sparkling little cafe with black-and-white checked wallpaper borders and crisp, white curtains at the windows. There are booths and tables, and a one-page menu for breakfast and lunch favorites. Cooking is home-style. If you want sophisticated city fare, come to the east entrance in the evenings. To watch the big game with your favorite brew, head in from the north. All three eateries use the same kitchen and maybe some of the same help. The clever owners are trying to get the most out of their investment.

The fine dining side was not open when we visited. The menu looks very impressive, however, and the chef has won accolades. This place seems to have great potential. If you like variety in familiar surroundings, Jordan's fits the bill.

Peppermill
Valentine

402-376-1440

You are really uptown when you visit the Peppermill in downtown Valentine. A glance at the dessert carousel alone is worth at least 500 calories, but we bet you can't just glance at this tempting array. This is western Nebraska's finest dessert spread; you've got to see and, better yet, sample the towering pies and cakes.

78

The restaurant itself is enormous—there's a beer garden with a sweetheart theme, a nod to the town name; a cavernous game room/bar in the back; and segregated dining rooms for smokers and nonsmokers. For under eight bucks, you can get scrumptious full-course meals in an inviting atmosphere with inventive specials so you won't get bored on repeat visits. Open for breakfast, lunch and dinner, the Peppermill without question draws them in from miles around. Second-generation Josephs, Betty and Bill, now run the place, and they keep a close eye on service and quality.

Across the street from the Peppermill is an attractive building that may have been an auto repair shop or filling station in its previous life. The Ambrosia Gardens (402-376-1927) was not open when we spent time in Valentine, but it's definitely filling a niche in this community. Picture a spotless decor of light wood and black accents—interesting, contemporary in feel with everything you'd want in a big-city coffee bar. There's latte, cappuccino, espresso, mocha, plus gourmet ice cream. We hope it's a big hit with the canoe crowd who come to do the Niobrara River, one of the nation's ten best canoe rivers according to *Backpacker* magazine.

Another attraction will be the Cowboy Trail, a hiker-biker trail built on an abandoned rail line. When finished, it will be the longest bicycle trail in the United States, and a sure draw for enthusiasts from throughout the country. An eatery like the Ambrosia Garden ought to hit the spot.

Snake Falls Canyon Restaurant   *402-376-3667*
Valentine

Anna and Bill Blatt are the luckiest couple in Nebraska; they live and work perched on the banks of Snake Falls Canyon. We mean that literally—they live and work in the same rustic wooden cabin that serves as the restaurant. And frankly, restaurant is too large a word. This is a snug little cabin with six or seven homemade booths, knotty-pine walls, a potbellied stove in the corner, and curtains straight out of the 1940s.

The Blatts are lucky because they are guardians of Snake Falls, located in a narrow canyon just twenty-three miles south of Valentine on Highway 97, or just a little north of Merritt Dam. For less than a dollar, you can walk down to the falls on steep, unimproved trails. The loose, sandy soil makes it a poor trip for the faint-hearted, but it's well worth the price of admission and the risk to life and limb for the nimble. Snake River is one of Nebraska's finest trout streams, with brown and rainbow trout swimming in the clear waters. In fact, record trout have been caught in this canyon.

A fishing and hunting club owns nearby cabins, and the members share with the Blatts one of the little-known treasures of the state. The restaurant is open seven days a week. Service is haphazard, but it's the only place for miles so relax and enjoy the ambience. It's obvious that when the restaurant isn't open, the couple lives right there in the restaurant. A doily-covered lounge chair in the corner is a good clue. If you walk in the back room, or living room, with its picture windows, you can shoot pool, have beer, and wait for your order to arrive. Gazing into the canyon while you wait is not a bad way to pass the time. If you're anywhere near Snake Falls Canyon, stop by.

"Everyone is famous in this town. And everyone is necessary. Townspeople go to the Vaughn grocery store for the daily news, and to the Home restaurant for history class, especially at evensong when the old people eat gravied pot roast and lemon meringue pies and calmly sip coffee from cups they tip to their mouths with both hands. The Kiwanis Club meets here on Tuesday nights, and hopes are made public, petty sins are tidily dispatched, and proceeds from the gumball machines are talleyed up and poured into the upkeep of a playground."

—from "Nebraska" by Ron Hansen

South Central

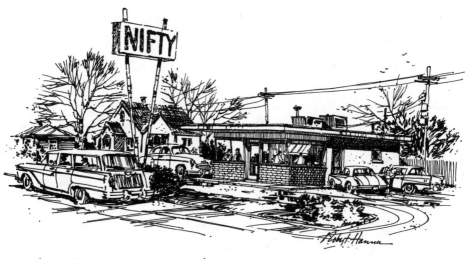

The Nifty Drive In - Grand Island, Ne.

Dowd's

308-382-4837

Alda

Dowd's is beef. Go for the big Sunday brunch. Founded by the same family who started Dreisbach's in Grand Island, Dowd's actually gets the nod over its famous cousin, some diners say. See what you think.

Korner Kafe

no phone

Byron

Downtown Byron isn't exactly booming. Like so many small towns, it's struggling but not going down without a fight. Years ago the community decided that it had to have a cafe. Locals formed a nonprofit organization, cleaned up an old tavern, recruited a staff, and opened the Korner Kafe. It's open daily, except Sunday, from 8 a.m. to 2 p.m.

When we visited six years ago, the servers' average age was 65. Now we'd guess the average is 71. They may be a little older, but they're just as friendly, and the food is just as good. The long tables recall harvest days on the farm. Ready for the rush, they were set with plates of fresh tomatoes when we arrived a half hour before noon. The Korner Kafe serves farm food, filling food, stick-to-the ribs food. The main dish comes with a full complement of side dishes. And there are usually two entrees served each day. Our heaping beef-noodle casserole was accompanied by peas and carrots, potato salad, Jell-O salad, two slices of bread, lemonade, and chocolate chip cheesecake or pudding. The price? $4.75.

We asked if community women still bring in the pies on Saturdays. Our waitress reported it was standing room only in the Korner Kafe just the week before when "eight pies disappeared."

Another told us that "people in small towns gather on the street corner and come in all at once." She was right; a Byron-sized stampede entered at noon. The place was nearly full as we got up to leave. When we paid our bill, the cook's daughter, a ten-year-old, placed our money in a cash register older than the servers and smiled as she told us good-bye. We left with full stomachs and warm feelings about this small town. Although there are many deserted buildings in Byron and the school is now closed, there's plenty of life here, and good food. The Korner Kafe lives on.

Brad's Supper Club
Franklin

715 15th Ave.
308-425-3289

What matters at Brad's Supper Club is steak, the United States of America, Husker football, and country music—not necessarily in that order.

Coney Island Lunch Room
Grand Island

104 East 3rd St.
308-382-7155

The Katrouzos family of Grand Island has made a name for itself in the hot dog hall of fame. In 1933 the Katrouzos family patriarch moved to Grand Island. A few weeks after arriving, he invested his life savings in a long, narrow storefront in downtown Grand Island. There he began serving hot dogs, better known as Coney Islands, similar to the ones that had been hawked along the beach at Coney Island in New York as early as 1871. He named his restaurant the Coney Island Lunch Room.

Ten years later son Gus took over for his father and the business has continued to thrive as a hot dog palace with a vivid personality. It's a Greek family affair. Gus, seventy-something, is still going strong, and other family members tend the tiny dining room.

The sign out front is so faded that the Lunch Room is easy to miss, but ask anyone in town; they've all been there. The forty-one-person capacity is strained at noon as loyal patrons line the long lunch counter and pack the row of booths. A counter seat is the most desirable. Seated there, a customer can watch the family, like square dancers, weave an elaborate dance behind the counter while delivering dogs and witty repartee to satisfied patrons. The house specialty, the Coney Island, is an all-beef wiener nestled in a fresh, soft bun. It's the topping that sets it off from your run-of-the-mill dogs. The sauce is a secret spicy chili liberally dressing the wiener; onion chunks top it off. Few customers can get by with just one—the Lunch Room sells about 300 Coneys each day.

The Coney Island Lunch Room offers a classic 1940s-style milk shake. You know how it goes—ice cream, flavoring, and milk dumped into a huge, shiny canister that mysteriously attaches itself to a whirring green mixer. Then the shake is poured into a large glass, which is placed before you along with the half-filled metal canister.

At the Coney Island Lunch Room in Grand Island, Gus is the tableside entertainment. He'll keep you in stitches while you chow down. Enjoy the atmosphere, as this is one of the last great places in the state.

Dreisbach's
Grand Island

1137 So. Locust St.
308-382-5450

The world's best steaks are served in the Midwest. It's here that cattle are fed the abundant grain required to produce steaks that are tender, succulent, and full of flavor. The large Midwest steakhouses gain the competitive edge in taste by buying whole sides of beef, hanging them in their own coolers for aging, and cutting them on the premises. Pre-cut, frozen beef just doesn't measure up to the aged genuine article.

There are lots of great steakhouses in Nebraska, but in central Nebraska, and especially among I-80 travelers, Dreisbach's in Grand Island is right up at the top. You can get any kind of steak imaginable at Dreisbach's. It can be custom cut to your specifications. Besides beef, seafood, including lobster, is served along with chicken and rabbit.

Your entree includes hot baking powder biscuits and honey, and lettuce salad with your choice of five kinds of homemade salad dressing. The dressings include a deadly, creamy garlic that will keep you in isolation for a week. Also try the sunflower potatoes, a cross between cheesy hash browns and crisp potato cakes. Yum!

The restaurant originated in 1932 in a two-story farmhouse. Its tradition of farm-style meals continues with heaping plates of all-you-can-eat fried chicken and bowls of mashed potatoes and vegetables.

As in most Nebraska steakhouses, the atmosphere in Dreisbach's is as plain as an I-80 truck stop. The service is usually efficient and sometimes gruff. But for beef—the kind that's hard to find outside the Midwest—Dreisbach's is the place. Dreisbach's is beef lover's heaven.

El Tapatio
Grand Island

2610 South Locust
308-381-4511

El Tapatio offers delicious fare from south of the border. The restaurant specializes in the cuisine of Guadalajara in Mexico. We're far from experts in this area, but folks who should know, tell us that El Tapatio is not to be missed. Cactus chicken is the dish mentioned most often. Expect big portions and full-course meals. This is not a taco stand or fast-food joint.

Fourth Street Cafe
Grand Island

414 West 4th St.
308-384-3448

On any given morning the Fourth Street Cafe is Grand Island's secret men's club. It'll be packed with men—suited men, blue-collar men, retired men—stoking up on sausage and coffee before attacking their day. We didn't see a single woman diner at the Fourth Street Cafe.

It's an intimate place; there's room for only thirty diners, and when things get crowded, it's like eating at a boardinghouse. Keep your elbows in, your feet under the table, and your voice down to a whisper if you're intending to pass atomic secrets, but holler if you need some catsup for the hash browns.

Ambience is not the attraction in this tiny, concrete-block cafe. Dining is casual—furnishings are nothing-matches, flea-market style. The inside is arranged in a no-nonsense manner, a reminder that you're not here for decoration, you're here to eat.

What's the attraction? That's a good question. Perhaps it's the honest, gritty feel of the place. The counter has a battered look from decades of hot plates and hot coffee. Perhaps it's the energy of the customers revving up for the day or the bustle and banter of the waitresses. Undoubtedly the noise, like the strong coffee, helps to jump-start the day. Or maybe it's the aroma, a nostalgic blend of grease and cigarette that seeps into your clothes and lingers as long as the taste of the sausage.

We had bacon and eggs, hash browns, toast, and coffee, plus a half order of biscuits and gravy—six bucks. Although we haven't tried it yet, the hash served on Saturdays draws uniform compliments from the regulars. How to describe the food? It's hearty, filling, manly food. It's simply pleasurable, don't-talk-to-me-about-calories-and-cholesterol grub. Go to the Fourth Street Cafe at least once. More often and you'll send your cardiologist into conniptions.

La Mexicana
Grand Island

111 E. 4th Street
308-381-4434

North of downtown a little ethnic outpost is bringing spice to the Grand Island food scene. In our cruise up and down Fourth Street we saw Asian markets, Laotian and Thai restaurants, Mexican cafes, and a Mexican bakery and deli, La Mexicana. Since the bakery-deli was the only spot open, we decided to give it a try.

First of all, this a self-service eatery. Walk to the counter and place your order. Signs will be posted in both English and Spanish. Non-Spanish speakers may feel a little lost, but someone will help explain the details of your order. Once your plate is filled, take your tray to the condiment bar for delicious choices: chopped, fresh cilantro, onions, pico de gallo, red and green chilies, peppers, and more. Get a cold drink from the cooler. Pick up something from the bakery case. The cashier is at the back of the store, but grab a table even before you check out. All the tables were occupied when we visited, and you'll want to relax to enjoy your food. There was a busy take-out service. Orders can be called in to be ready when you arrive.

The chile Colorado was delicious. It was a full meal with beans, rice, and four flour tortillas. The chile was a flavorful, spicy stew. Hot, but not a four-alarm blaze. Our meal was satisfying, and it was fun to visit a very casual, neighborhood place. Think Hispanic convenience store. Patrons can also pick up groceries and household supplies. We don't know enough to call it authentic food from south of the border, but all the people eating there seemed more than satisfied.

Nonna's Palazzo   *820 West 2nd St.*
Grand Island   *308-384-3029*

Nonna's is an American dream. Chiarra Brazzale, the restaurant's namesake, grew up in Italy where she dreamed of coming to America. In 1914 her dream came true. She immigrated to the United States, landing in Sunrise, Wyoming, where she set up a boardinghouse. Most of her roomers were Italian men who worked in the iron mines nearby, and she cooked hearty food from the old country to please these lonely workers.

Chiarra Brazzale's granddaughter, Fran Schaffer, used to visit her nonna (Italian for grandmother) in Wyoming. While working with her during these visits, Fran learned the secrets of Italian cooking. Like her nonna, Fran also had a dream. Growing up in Grand Island, Fran and her brother would often walk by what they considered the most magnificent home in the world, the Hamilton-Donald House. "It was the only house in Grand Island that I ever wanted," she says. "It was so majestic-looking."

In 1983 Fran's dream came true. She and her husband purchased the house and moved their family into the up-stairs rooms. Fran retired from nursing and fulfilled the rest of her dream—to carry on the Italian cooking tradition inspired by her grandmother.

She named her restaurant Nonna's Palazzo. Palazzo means *palace,* and the name fits, for the house is a mansion. Built in 1905 by banker Ellsworth D. Hamilton, the three-story, white house, an example of the neoclassic revival style, is now listed on the National Register of Historic Places.

Meals are served in the living room to the left of the foyer as you enter, and in the dining room to the right. The furnish-ings are antique pieces that Fran has collected over the years. Soft classical music in the background enhances the elegant atmosphere.

Fran is the only cook, and from the quality of her fare, it is clear that Nonna was a great tutor. State-of-the-art, home-made pasta is the house specialty. Entrees feature mostly northern Italian cuisine—not just the tomato-based sauces from the south. A menu designates low-cholesterol selec-tions and includes daily specials.

In spite of the gourmet quality and the elegance of the surroundings, you'll be amazed at the reasonable prices. Like Nonna and Fran, we dream of returning to Nonna's.

Edwardian Lady Tea Room & Curiosity Shop
Grand Island   *920 West Third*
                                                    308-382-2229

Plum Thicket Tea Room & Gift Shop   *822 West First*
Grand Island   *308-384-6140*

Tearooms are blossoming in Grand Island. Smack dab in the middle of Nebraska, the Victorian era is in full bloom. Both the Edwardian Lady and Plum Thicket tearooms serve gourmet coffees and teas. The Edwardian Lady serves both high and low teas; sorry, no middle tea available. Light gourmet lunches, perfect for the ladies-who-lunch bunch, are available at both of these elegant, historic homes. These cozy tearooms are gentle additions to the community.

Plantation   *402-257-2188*
Guide Rock

In 1994 Guide Rock was one of seven communities in the nation named one of the *Best Small Towns in America*. Volunteers mowed, planted, painted, and repaired. New businesses opened, and old ones renovated and expanded. One of the town's leaders, Diana Vogler, co-owner of the new Plantation Restaurant, proclaims that the entrepreneurial spirit is alive and well in Guide Rock.

The Plantation reflects this same spirit. It's a beautiful building with a plush interior; the food is solid Nebraska steakhouse fare. Look over Guide Rock. It's a proud, prosperous small town. Be sure to stop at the Plantation. Both the town and the restaurant are a treat.

Black Dog Diner
Harvard

402-772-2074

Although not exactly the Ivy League, the Black Dog Diner in Harvard has developed a solid reputation for good food. Owned by the former county sheriff, the Black Dog is clean and bright with an Indian motif. The hot turkey sandwich and three-meat sub were delicious and filling. They served soup and salad as well as bread pudding and coconut pie for dessert. It's solid, substantial food, and lots better than the food served in cafeterias anywhere in the Ivy League.

La Mejicana
Hastings

627 W. 1st St.
402-463-0606

When nearly everyone involved in a Mexican restaurant is family, you know the food is going to be good. Mary Lou Alfaro and her family own and operate La Mejicana. Mary Lou says the specialty of the house is "authentic Mexican food"—and she's right. As you read down the menu, you'll find traditional Mexican-American fare, such as nachos, quesadilla, tostadas, chile verde, and flautas. But go to the next page. There you'll find dishes unavailable at a fast-food franchise. Mary Lou steps south of the border to cook family recipes with an authentic, delicious twist. There are carnitas (fried pork Mexican-style), steak ranchero (sirloin steak smothered in a spicy sauce and topped with Mexican sausage), camarones a la diablo (shrimp sauteed in red chile sauce), and pescado a la Veracruzana (fish filet with tomatoes, onions, bell peppers, and olives).

The restaurant is in a large, restored building on the edge of downtown. The atmosphere is bright and cheery, the service is friendly, and Mary Lou can cook "muy bueno!"

Zephyr Cafe

Holdrege

308-995-5774

Someone in Holdrege is restoring the old town depot. If you come for a visit, don't miss the Zephyr Cafe right across the street. This is a little cafe that pays tribute to the heyday of train travel. Passengers could get a bite while waiting for the train. Remember the California Zephyr? It used to steam right through here.

The owners have changed through the years, and the cafe quality has varied. New operators promise a few changes: all baked goods from scratch, for one; spiffing up the restroom, for another. If Dwayne Wagg is as good as his word, new things may be in store for the old Zephyr Cafe. And as long as his mother, Doris Peterson, is willing to get up early and bake for the cafe, things may be looking up in Holdrege. Townspeople anticipate changes that are long overdue. We're hoping that the Zephyr Cafe will get on track and keep rolling for the long haul.

Alley Rose

Kearney

2013 Central Ave.
308-234-1261

When we wrote our first book, no Kearney restaurants were included. Since then several fine eateries have sprung up. Alley Rose is one of them. Plushly decorated, highlighted with brass and dark woodwork, Alley Rose offers fine dining with excellent service.

The salad bar is a good one with homemade dressings. Our favorite was peppercorn-Parmesan cheese. Prime rib is a specialty and comes in three sizes. Ours was an incredibly tender piece of beef with delicious aroma and flavor. Plenty of food comes with your entree: freshly baked bread, salad bar, choice of potato, rice, or vegetable. If you want something other than beef, there's seafood, chicken, pasta, catfish, and many other tasty items. Alley Rose leads Kearney's culinary comeback.

The Cellar
Kearney

3901 2nd Ave.
308-236-6541

The locals swear by this walkout basement bar and grill. They report it has "no gimmicks, just good food and good service at reasonable prices." Another says it's "one of Kearney's best-kept secrets; it grew from a neighborhood bar to a world-renowned restaurant." Of course, that last boast came from the Chamber of Commerce, but see what you think.

Downhome Gourmet
Kearney

115 West 15th St.
308-237-0753

A Kearney area ranch family decided to cut out the middle man and market its quality Limousin beef directly to the consumer. Limousin is a lean, muscular breed popular in France and imported to this country a couple of decades ago.

The Downhome Gourmet is located in a small building just off the main street leading north to the downtown area. Although they market ranch-fresh beef products for take-home preparation, better let them do the cooking for you in Wonderful Waldo, their big smoker parked out front. It slow cooks the beef, using southern hickory and native apple wood. The Downhome Gourmet is takeout only; we sampled the barbecued beef sandwich. It was tender, smoky, and drenched in barbecue sauce. There are also delicious pork and beef ribs. The sides include cowboy Carl's three-bean baked beans, the 1995 first prize in the Nebraska new food products contest. They're smoked in a tangy sauce. If you like baked beans, you'll love this recipe.

Bravo to this ranch family for successfully taking the beef-marketing bull by the horns!

The French Cafe
Kearney

2202 Central Ave.
308-234-6808

One of our favorites for a mid-morning snack or gourmet lunch is the French Cafe in downtown Kearney. Decorated in a green-and-white picnic theme with small Parisian sidewalk tables, it's an inviting place to savor creative cooking. Offerings include quiches, croissants, salads, fruit plates, and a few heartier dishes like fettuccine Alfredo and lasagna. Check out the gourmet grilled cheese sandwich— a triple decker with marbled rye bread, Swiss, American, jack, and cheddar cheese grilled to perfection, and topped with yet another cheese, Parmesan. Cheese lovers will say "magnifique!" Lovers of pastries and pies will just nod and mumble; their mouths will be too full to speak.

Habɘtat
Kearney

121 W. 46th St.
308-237-2405

Habɘtat is a tribute to Nebraska's abundant wildlife and good food. Reminders of Nebraska's natural beauty fill this restful, upscale restaurant on the north edge of Kearney. A hand-painted mural, a marsh filled with sandhill cranes, geese, and ducks, washes across four walls of the Platte River room, highlighting the abundant waterfowl of the Kearney area. The room includes a huge stone fireplace.

Fishing is the theme of the patio room. Mounted trophy bass, old fishing creels, and colorful fishing lures decorate the room furnished with wicker. The ceiling is weathered barn siding. Large picture windows bring nature inside. There's a view of Lost Lake behind the restaurant. In the spring diners can watch newly hatched mallards swimming behind their parents.

Food is also a strong suit at the Habətat. Owners Jim Gardner and Larry Snyder bring lots of restaurant experience to the table, and the results show. Larry is owner of the successful Steak House in Lincoln, and Jim operates nine Country Kitchens. The creativity of manager Jeff Daley is evident in a wide range of creative dishes, unusual for this area. There's an oversized, onion-ring loaf with Dijon mustard, Cajun turkey quesadillas, Thai chicken pasta, baby back ribs, and Nebraska steaks. Habətat also promotes Nebraska agriculture. Once they featured prime rib: *Every Night's Prime Time for Prime Rib at the Habətat.* Really hungry? Tie into a twenty-two-ounce monster slab of prime rib. Steamed fresh vegetables, a rare treat—unforgivably rare, in most Midwest restaurants—was an accompaniment. Bravo!

The service is solicitous and speedy; the food unique and well made. Featured in a 1995 issue of *Midwest Living*, the Habətat is an excellent restaurant. If we lived near Kearney, we'd be there often enough to become part of the natural environment. The veggies and the view alone would bring us back again and again.

Simply Desserts
Kearney

2318 First Avenue
308-236-8288

Elegance meant to be shared is the motto of Simply Desserts. This new coffeehouse has plenty to share. There is every imaginable kind of gourmet coffee from cappuccino to caffe latte. And for desserts, there are thirty-three kinds of pies, twenty-six kinds of cheesecakes, thirty-six tortes, coffee cakes, cookies, muffins, scones, and breads. We sampled several offerings, including chocolate chip cookies, and agreed that someone here knows how to bake. Oh yes, at the bottom of the flyer, it says you can ask for the "fat-free goodies." We wonder what that could be.

Tex's Cafe
Kearney

23 East 21st
308-234-3949

Tex's Cafe is a country cafe that lost its way and decided to sit a spell in Kearney. Bill Ross of Kearney aptly describes its decor as nondescript. He's right: linoleum floor, metal chairs, Naugahyde booths, oil cloths, a Dr. Pepper clock, and Coca-Cola cooler. The colors are a far-from-soothing orange and blue. The highlights of this near-dive are the signs, such as In Case Of Fire, Remain Calm and Stay Seated Until All Employees Have Left The Building. One waitress is so thin, she couldn't eat there, but the cook obviously does.

A breakfast destination for downtowners, the cafe fills five or six tables with regular patrons. The general level of conversation goes something like: "What do you think of the strike?" "What strike?" "The baseball strike." "You get three, don't you?"

The specials are on a bulletin board; eggs and hashbrowns are sizzling on the grill; and six kinds of pies are chilling in the refrigerator. It's local color at its best.

J and J's City Cafe
Minden

413 N. Colorado
308-832-2788

The owners of J and J's City Cafe report that what makes them unique "...is not trying to be unique. It's just midwestern American cuisine." After you've tied into one of the sticky pecan rolls that seduce the unwary, you might disagree with the owners. These rolls are far from run-of-the-mill. If you want more plain old midwestern cuisine, try co-owner Jan Landrigan's hot beef sandwich with potatoes and gravy or the cream puffs. One of our favorites is the J and J burger. It's ground beef, Swiss cheese, smoked ham, lettuce, and a special sauce much better than any McSauce on the market. This is low-key chow stripped to the bare essentials—tasty home cooking at a low overhead price.

CJ's
Osceola

402-747-6441

Luncheon specials, rolls on the counter, pay-as-you-pour coffee, metal chairs, plain tables, some attempt at decor (a shelf of antiques running along one side of the dining room), pleasant service, low prices, and plain and plentiful food. That's CJ's, Polk County's contribution to blue plate America.

Little Mexico
Republican City

308-799-3205

If you can't stand the heat, don't try the green chile soup at Little Mexico. It'll make your brow sweat, your tongue catch fire, and your nostrils smoke. It's so hot they ought to serve it with flares and traffic cones. But it's good. Filled with chunks of chicken, chilies, jalapenos, and tomatoes, it'll put fire in your belly and have you singing love songs to your senorita on the way home.

We love hot Mexican food. Evidently the folks around Republican City do, too, because Little Mexico plays to a standing-room-only crowd on weekends. It's been an area favorite since 1975.

Not everything is as hot as the soup. The guacamole is mild, and nachos can be dipped in either mild or hot sauce. But if you crave more heat, nachos come with a side bowl of jalapenos. The original chips and salsa are addictive, and there are the standard Mexican favorites. The Mexican food is not as authentic as you can get in Scottsbluff, south Omaha, or Grand Island, but it's tasty. If you want to play it cool, enjoy the more typical Nebraska entrees of chicken, shrimp, and steak.

Jan's Strang Tavern   402-759-4834
Strang

Jan's is a small-town tavern with a big burger, a huge steak, and a varied menu. The sandwiches sound like a singing group: the Philly, Hawaiian, Western, and Strang Supreme. The latter puts the tavern on the map and is rated as one of the best burgers in the state. It combines beef with cheese, mushrooms, and Canadian bacon. They also have a thirty-two-ounce porterhouse. That's the biggest steak we've found in our travels. Open seven days a week from 7 a.m. to midnight, the Strang Tavern is worth finding. It's north of Bruning, east of Ong, and west of Ohiowa.

Aunt Ruth's
Stromsburg

402-764-4937

Located in the country just one mile north and two and three-fourths miles west of Stromsburg, Aunt Ruth's Tea Room and Gift Shoppe is worth a drive out of your way. This is the restored 1882 home of the Sundberg clan, immigrants from Sweden. The house has remained in the family all these years. Rather than let it sit unused when the family moved to a modern home on the property, they restored it. You'll have to drive up the lane past the modern home to reach Aunt Ruth's little two-story house in the middle of the farmyard.

Aunt Ruth's serves light luncheon fare by reservation only on Wednesday and Friday. Just one entree is served and new menus are created week by week. There'll be a sandwich or hearty salad main course served with fruit and a muffin or nut bread on the side. Chicken chow mein salad and smoked turkey on pumpernickel were a couple of the offerings one month. Gather a group and head on out to lunch for a special celebration. They'll arrange to serve at other times if you prefer. Call for details. On snowy days horse-drawn sleigh rides can be arranged.

If you're in the neighborhood, you can simply stop by for coffee and dessert 1-5 p.m. Tuesday through Saturday. With a mug of coffee you can browse from attic to cellar. The history of this charming house, the home of a real Aunt Ruth, is an engaging story. The furnishings are all original, just as it was in Aunt Ruth's day. Kudos to the Sundbergs for preserving this farmstead and for sharing family memories.

Explore awhile and find the lovely country Swedish church in the nearby village of Swede Home. For the curious, there's a unique house made from an old railroad passenger car just one-half mile east of Aunt Ruth's. Don't miss it!

The Big Idea Cafe

402-773-4321

Sutton

Although Bev Griess quit teaching school, she's still an educator. Only now she educates the palates of Sutton. This woman can cook anything—and often does just that. Some happy customers may not know what they're eating, but they come back just the same. She may serve a German special one day and a Swedish one the next. She may serve Hungarian goulash, Polish pierogis, or Austrian turnovers just to keep them off balance. And when her customers think they've tried just about everything, she'll bring out plain meat loaf and mashed potatoes. She keeps them guessing in Sutton, but nobody's complaining.

There's no menu at the Big Idea. Bev dreams up her culinary potpourri once a month and prints it on the placemats, supplemented by a chalkboard behind the counter. She does serve the usual beef, pork, and chicken, but transforms them from the mundane to the sublime. At the Big Idea, for example, it's chicken strata, not fried chicken; it's barbecue steak, not baked steak; a croissant becomes a German croissant, and humble pepperoni pizza is transformed into a customer favorite—fruit pizza.

On Friday Bev allows her customers to step off the culinary roller coaster with a special offering of soup, sandwich, and a salad bar. But that, too, is different each week.

Bev's an inventor who serves up one great food idea after another. Frankly, her motto that *There's More To Eating Than Burgers* is truly a big idea for many small towns. The Big Idea is nothing fancy, but neither are the prices. It's quality food, creative with a twist.

Chances R

York

124 West 5th

402-362-7755

Chances R continues to grow and improve. The Shultz family started it as the Cozy Lunch seating only fifty in 1937. In 1957 the Shultz's daughter and son-in-law, Shirley and Raymond Reetz, purchased it. Now it seats 550.

The formula: consistency, high quality, reasonable prices, and variety in atmosphere. As the restaurant grew, four distinct areas emerged. The east area is a casual setting; the main dining room is more formal; the lounge, with colorful stained glass, a giant stone fireplace, and polished brass, provides an elegant warm ambience. Our favorite area is the Tommy-Suz Beer Garden. It looks like a big old garage transformed into an indoor beer garden. The furnishings include huge tree-trunk tables with log chairs, antiques, gas pumps, and old signs—neon and otherwise.

The beer garden is home to one of the largest Sunday brunches in the Western Hemisphere. Table after table is loaded with more food than several football teams could consume. The variety is overwhelming. There are custom-made omelettes, Belgian waffles, orange roughy in butter almondine sauce, salads galore, beef and ham, and tables piled with desserts. And that only hits the highlights. Go hungry and don't plan to eat again for a week.

Specialties in the main dining area include pan-fried chicken, barbecued pork ribs, steaks galore, and a surprising variety of fish and seafood from trout and crab legs to lobster tails.

The owners of Chances R have received the Restaurateur of the Year Award from their Nebraska colleagues. They well deserved it.

In The Cafe

Here in the cafe this morning
we're discussing the world or we're quiet.
The cafe lets us in, the door squeaks open
long and loose like a string of spiderweb
in a curve of breeze. The door
slaps shut. The cafe
lets us in, holds us,

gives us a table, give us coffee, gives us
heavy brown cups of chocolate.
We talk to someone or we sit
alone, reading, thinking. On the wall
the arms of the philodendron are a Victorian
lady, fainting. A man walks by on
the sidewalk, the sun making shadows of his
eyes. At ten a.m. Rosie washes the tables,
makes the rounds. Once she laid her hand

on the shoulder of a woman
crying quietly at a table, writing
in a notebook. Small cool anvil,
Rosie's hand. The floor boards of the cafe
creak under boots and sandals. The plants
in the window do not
fuss. They yellow a leaf
and drop it, all in good time.

—Marjorie Saiser

Southwest

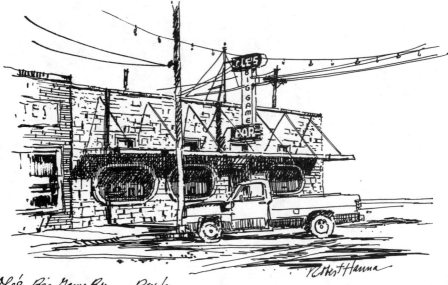

Ole's Big Game Bar - Paxton

Robert Hanna

Little Deuce Coupe
Cozad

141 E. 8th St.
308-784-5050

This new arrival in Cozad is a fifties replica. There's a soda fountain on one side with black-and-white linoleum tiles on the floor and classic furniture—aluminum and Formica with turquoise and pink seat covers. The menu is typical fountain fare. Hours are offbeat; call ahead. The other side of the building is a showroom for restored automobiles. Cruise it to see both antique and classic models. When you come to Cozad, you can browse the attractions down the block too. There's the Robert Henri museum and the 100th Meridian museum next door to a great, old art deco movie theater that's still in use.

PJ's
Cozad

103 E. Monroe St.
308-784-4777

When focusing on food, there's nothing more distracting than a loud conversation at the next table. It was particularly annoying when one of us was drawing a bead on a Greek salad, a rarity in western Nebraska, and savoring a toasted grinder sandwich of meats and cheeses while the other was waiting for a pizza baked in a stone-bottom oven.

But that's just what happened at PJ's. A large man at the next table interrupted our reverie with lip smacks, moans, and sighs. Annoyed, we turned to see what was causing the culinary consternation. He was devouring a large slice of cream pie.

As we watched the pie disappear, we wondered what kind it was. "This is heaven, heavenly pie," he thundered. "They call it butterscotch dream pie, but I call it heaven." Ignoring the tasty food before us, we quickly ordered a slice and ate it before finishing the rest of our meal. It was worth it—smooth filling with caramel-like butterscotch taste and as flaky as crust can be. "It's fabulous, isn't it?" our neighbor exclaimed. We could only nod in agreement; we were still enjoying the last crumbs.

Made by the family grandmother from her own recipes, the pies originally were brought to the restaurant every day. Today, however, the recipe is in the hands of younger pastry chefs who have continued the tradition. Some years ago a food writer for the *Los Angeles Times* stopped at PJ's for a snack and tried the butterscotch dream pie. Hooked, the writer lauded the pie in his paper and the recipe was sent out nationwide on the AP wire—a transcontinental treat.

If you can hold off on the pie, enjoy a variety of entrees at this popular family restaurant. They serve exotic treats such as crab legs and lobster, but the hoagie, pizza, pasta, and pie are what we recommend.

Yellow Rose
Curtis

116 Center
308-367-5620

There's plenty of room at the Yellow Rose. With a combined dining room and lounge, this place can hold a full house. Open seven days a week from 7:00 a.m. until 1:00 a.m., it serves a full menu and specialties. The namesake can be found on table tops and elsewhere.

Enjoy specials—Friday, crab legs; Saturday, prime rib; Sunday, a noon buffet, and Mexican later in the afternoon.

The Pool Hall

Eustis

Everything about the Pool Hall in Eustis is unique—history, decor, owner, food, menu, music.

History: The Pool Hall was built in 1904. Yet six years later it was targeted for destruction by Carrie Nation, the Kansas temperance crusader. She warned the owner that she would bring three hundred ax-wielding women to turn the "infernal old whiskey shop into kindling." Her arrest in Kansas saved the Pool Hall. Seven years later it was ravaged by fire, to be rebuilt in 1918.

Decor: The building has high, pressed-tin ceilings, wood floors, brick walls, a beautiful oak back bar, and, of course, pool tables. The brick walls are covered with pink flamingos, antiques, and mirrors. Expansion to the east into the former boardinghouse/hotel is planned. There'll be a few rooms for rent, a banquet room, and a special section for snooker.

Owner: Constance Koch grew up nine miles south of Eustis and remembers going to the Pool Hall with her father as a little girl. She says, "It was always filled with men smoking cigars, cigarettes, and pipes; chewing tobacco and spitting on the floor or in the spittoons; drinking beer; shooting snooker; and playing cribbage or pitch. But the thing I remember most is the candy counter and the old man named Charlie Heiser who always bought me a Cherry Mash and an orange pop." Those childhood memories stayed with Connie and in 1976, at age 23, she bought the Pool Hall. Her management skill and creativity are obvious.

Music: The background music isn't top forties or country music. Connie plays blues and says her customers like it.

Food: Connie decided to serve something a little different. She settled on Mexican, and it's been a great choice. Mexican fare includes chile rellenos, a fried, cheese-stuffed chili pepper smothered with your choice of mild red, hot, or special hot green chilies. Look for tamales, burritos, fajitas, and huevos rancheros. Other unique eats are the fresh Platte River shrimp dinner, a Polish sausage sandwich (great after hunting), and the unusual appetizer, corn nuggets—creamed sweet corn, breaded and deep fried. Margaritas come in four flavors and colors. Check out the Pool Hall's unusual theme menus, ranging from astrology to the Wizard of Oz to old newspapers. They're a fun read.

Thank goodness the Pool Hall has survived all these years. It's a classy watering hole in a great little town. A toast to Carrie Nation who spared the Pool Hall and to Connie Koch who's made it thrive.

Butch's Bar   *308-368-7231*
Hershey

One of our fantasies is to own a Sandhills ranch. It would be a ranch in the hills north of Hershey. At least once a week for the rest of our lives we'd clean up after a hard day of working cattle and drive into Butch's Bar for a great hunk of beefsteak. We'd be able to call the bartender and our favorite waitress by name. The minute we walked in he'd order our favorite beverage, and she would know, without asking, that on that night we wanted a T-bone for two, medium rare, and a basket of fabulous fries, piping hot and salty. And they'd warn us right away if, for some reason, the kitchen was out of our favorite dessert.

Butch's was a small bar when we first wrote about it. It's now greatly enlarged. It's lost some of its charm—the flashing sign that said "Now serving breakfast" is gone. But its beef is still nothing but quality. There's a bar on one side and a dining room on the other. The dining room has a plain, no-nonsense air, as if reminding you that what you came to do is eat.

And eat big you will. Butch's is not for wimps. No delicate quiches or mesclun drizzled in vinaigrette here. We've seen some big cowboys eating huge steaks at Butch's, and they always look satisfied. Follow their lead, and you will be, too.

The prime rib is the house specialty, but we prefer the twenty-four-ounce sirloin for two. It's a great, charred hunk with the flavor of perfectly aged, grain-fed beef. Thick. Tender. Swimming in juices. It's so good that ardent carnivores will find themselves gnawing on the bone and covering themselves with greasy goodness.

Rocket Inn
308-364-9906

Indianola

For more than forty years, the folks in southwest Nebraska have been crowding into the Rocket Inn. The attraction is a distinctive, authentic Italian-style pizza served only on Wednesday and Friday nights. The family recipe made its way to Indianola from Italy when Bob Blume brought his bride, Fiorella, back to Indianola after serving in the armed forces. As it turns out, a most valuable item in her dowry was the family pizza recipe. The inn began serving pizza before local folks knew what it was. It didn't take long for local taste buds to get well acquainted with this novel concoction.

The Rocket Inn pizza is distinctive. It has a thin crust, loads of cheese and meat, and no tomato sauce. The toppings range from the typical pepperoni, hamburger, and sausage to sauerkraut. You might even be able to get peanut butter!

Present owners, George and Sue Cornwell, have continued the successful pizza formula and have expanded into other areas. Pizza is just one of the goodies served at the inn. It's open for all meals. The dinners, including steaks and chicken, come with a salad bar, potato, and Texas toast. There are delicious luncheon specials, too. You might want to try the pickles. We did. They come highly recommended. We more than paid for our meal at this little cafe with a winning pickle card.

Dotty's Diner   *604 N. Washington*
Lexington   *308-324-2036*
The Leprechaun   *West Highway 30*
Lexington   *308-324-4597*

We were stunned to hear of the closing of Lexington's nationally-famous cafe, Little Paris, but the cafe's owners needed more family time and they reluctantly closed down.

In consultation with the Paris family, we've found two other local spots to help take the edge off your appetite. After all, we can't have you stopping for fast food as you make your way along the great Platte River road.

Dotty's is a breakfast and lunch place, open from early morning through noon. It's a little lunch counter with a few tables. You can have breakfast, a coffee break, or a noon meal of sandwiches and soups. It does have homemade pies and rolls, a good reason to draw a bead on Dotty's when hunger strikes.

You might also want to try the Leprechaun, especially if you're coming through town on the 17th. For on this day, no matter what the month, it's St. Patrick's Day with a corned beef and cabbage special. The Irish theme is obvious. The decorations won't surprise you. This, too, is a lunch counter with tables, although it's a little larger and it serves early evening meals. We mean really early; they close at 7:00 p.m. The evening menus consist of typical dinner choices—a couple of steaks and sandwiches, too. The pies are made right on the premises.

The Brick Wall

North Platte

507 No. Dewey
308-532-7545

Sometimes folks outside of the big cities are reluctant to try new foods. That's particularly true in the Great Plains. We rely too much—sometimes to the point of boredom—on steak, burgers, and chicken. Marcene Franzen agreed and decided to do something different. It takes a handful of innovation and an armload of courage to start a restaurant in western Nebraska that serves such interesting and delicious dishes as zesty lemon chicken, chicken and mushroom crepes, asparagus quiche, veggie fettuccine, crab Alfredo, and spinach salad with raspberry dressing—BRAVO! And if you want burgers, she has them—albeit jazzed up a bit.

And that's only part of the lunch menu. Get there in the a.m. and try an omelette made to order with a selection of sixteen fillings. There's also orange french toast and apple scrapple (a sausage, cornmeal loaf enhanced with diced apples, fried, and served with two eggs and warm maple syrup). Mother Endacott served a similar dish we called panhaus. There's a bacon-rice dish, and the list goes on and on.

And then we come to Marcene's "outrageous sundaes." How about a Black Bart: chocolate ice cream with a hot fudge, marshmallow topping, almonds, and a cookie? Or the Hawaiian fantasy—vanilla ice cream in a sea of chunky pineapple, coconut, and bananas with white caps of whipped cream and macadamia nuts. Need we say more?

The ambience is a further reflection of Plains creativity. She remodeled an early 1900s building, but preserved its unique features. The brick wall to the south was discovered during the remodeling process. The old wood floor was retained, and light fixtures from the old McCabe Hotel were installed. The booths were fashioned from oak shipping crates. Flowered wallpaper and craft wall hangings add a homey touch.

Marcene has a talent for conjuring up wonderful combinations. Once the customers taste her culinary inventions, steak, burgers, and chicken become just a distant memory.

Doris' Tavern
North Platte

404 No. Dewey
308-532-5000

Doris Dotson was only sixteen and too young to be a volunteer at the legendary North Platte depot canteen, a stopover for troop trains carrying service personnel across the country during World War II. So she and her friends entertained them. They jitterbugged with the soldiers in the depot waiting room before the train whistle beckoned them back on board.

When Doris and husband, Wayne, bought this downtown bar about ten years ago, the previous owner had hung photos of forty-five North Platte area servicemen and women. Now there are 580 pictures of veterans from the North Platte area. The south wall is almost covered.

Doris' Bar, a bit battered and tattered these days but still loaded with charm, was once the dining room for the fancy McCabe Hotel in the thirties and forties. Many a brew has been tipped at the bar's padded rail, now cracking and peeling with age. At the far end of the lounge is a glass block wall with red lights shining through, a fifties remnant. At a large round table in the back corner, the regulars gather nightly to play cocklebur, a pitchlike card game.

Doris is now a beautiful woman in her sixties. Fifty years ago, the boys must have battled for a chance to dance with her. To this day, Doris glows when she shares her memories of dancing in the depot and shows her collection of photographs, obviously her most prized possession.

Cassel's Family Restaurant
Ogallala

S. of I-80 Exit
308-284-2088

Sometimes when we're cruising the Interstate, we get a hankering for cakes—pancakes. And when we do, there's only one place to pull over and fuel up—Cassel's in Ogallala.

Following the successful formula of a family restaurant, where the owners are always on hand, Cassel's has survived for over twenty-five years. You have to serve an awful lot of good pancakes to an awful lot of satisfied customers to make it that long.

There's a full menu for all three meals, but pancakes are the draw. Specialties include peanutty chocolate pancakes, German apple pancakes (browned popovers puffed and topped with spiced apples), and orange-blossom crepes (thin strawberry pancakes drizzled with a delicate orange sauce). They all share a wondrous fluffy lightness that takes family in the kitchen to prepare.

Hilltop Inn
Ogallala

Near Kingsley Dam
308-284-4534

For dining, one of the best views in Nebraska is from the Hilltop Inn. We were last there at sundown on a late summer evening. We arrived early enough to request a prime table looking west out the row of picture windows onto thousands of acres of water—Lake McConaughy. What a floor show! The sunset was spectacular. It couldn't have been any prettier if we'd been sitting on the west coast of Ireland.

The food—standard Nebraska steakhouse fare—was almost as good as the view. We'll go back again for both.

Homemade Heaven Sandwich Shop
Ogallala

308-284-4879

You're heading down I-80, kind of in a hurry. Can't stomach the usual fast-food fare? Pull off at Ogallala, drive across the viaduct, take a left and go about two blocks. Stop. You're at Homemade Heaven. The crew there will fix you a sandwich that'll make you think you've gone to heaven. It's the best sandwich shop on the Interstate, with thirty-two different sandwich combinations. The Reuben, for example, is served on a large bun with thick, juicy layers of corned beef, sauce, and two kinds of cheese.

The soups are great. We settled on ham and bean after wavering over three other selections. The big, steamy bowl was thick with chunks of tender ham, swimming in beans.

Located on the main east-west street, Homemade Heaven is also open in the morning for coffee, muffins, and rolls. It's one of the best-kept secrets on the Interstate. We would trade two McDonald's, a KFC, and a first-round draft pick for lunch at this excellent sandwich shop.

Ole's Big Game Lounge

Paxton

308-239-4500

At Ole's Big Game Lounge, world-famous, big-game hunter Ole Herstadt has assembled one of the largest private collections of big-game trophies in the world—over two hundred in all. In addition to a huge standing polar bear, there are elephant, giraffe, buffalo, leopard, elk, jaguar, python, and, of course, the rare Nebraska jackelope. Ole's looks like a hunting lodge with trophies mounted on rustic, knotty-pine walls. Non-hunters cringe, and animal rights activists ought to stay clear; the decor represents an era when the conservation of animals was not a high priority.

Opened August 9, 1933, the day Prohibition ended, Ole's is the source of many stories. Tom Allen, esteemed writer for the *Omaha World-Herald*, recounts the time he was assigned to cover the dedication of Chuchi the polar bear. Ole poured pink champagne over its nose. By coincidence, the dedication included a bunch of cowhands in town recuperating from a cattle drive. A brawl broke out—"straight out of a John Wayne movie." When Ole saw things were getting out of hand, he grabbed an ax handle, stood on the bar, and yelled, "Everybody out back. No fighting in the bar." The fighting stopped, the combatants moved outside, and the melee started again. After a while, Ole'd had enough. "OK, that's it. Stop your fighting. Drinks are on the house." It worked. The fight stopped, and the cowpokes trooped back inside and bellied up to the bar as if nothing had happened. The trail boss explained to Ole, "The boys were blowing off steam. They'll be no more trouble." The two bullet holes in the floor are remnants from a 1938 incident. Obviously, another story.

When Ole retired in 1988, he first sold the bar to two young locals. Because it was touted as "Nebraska's Most Famous

Watering Hole," Ole just couldn't stand to see the bar close and the collection scattered. When current owner, farmer Jim Holzfaster, bought the place, he had no experience in the bar and restaurant business. But he loved Ole's because he spent hours there playing pool as a child, supervised by Ole's mother.

The trophy collection remains intact, and Holzfaster has made some dramatic improvements in the menu. In the old days, the only grub you could get at Ole's was a hot dog and a hard-boiled egg. With a new kitchen Ole's now serves a complete menu at reasonable prices. The steaks, cut fresh daily, are excellent. They also offer buffalo burgers, labeled the delicacy of the Plains, and Rocky Mountain oysters so good you'll go nuts over them, and the ever-faithful hot dog, ironically, the only edible stuffed animal in the place. You gotta see Ole's.

Country Inn   *no phone*
Wellfleet

The Country Inn is a mobile home turned country cafe. Singularly economical in decoration, the inn obviously doesn't attract customers with its looks; they come to eat. Four walls, ten tables, and a good meal on wheels—that's the Country Inn.

The Country Inn's owners, Debbie and Jerry Horton, moved to Nebraska about five years ago. Debbie had been a trucker and Jerry had raised worms. Before purchasing the cafe, the couple started a candy business, Debbie's Delights. They made an arrangement with the former owner of the cafe to come in at night and use the stoves to cook the candies. Six years ago the owner said they might as well buy the building, so they did. With hard work, determination, and "madness" they've developed successful enterprises with both the candy business and the cafe.

When asked what makes the cafe unique, Debbie reports "that it ain't fancy and neither are we. We're a roadside cafe in a little trailer. On Sunday people wait in their cars until we call them in. Sometimes it gets pretty confusing hollering out that front door. People have waited an hour to get in here."

Last time we visited we had the chicken-fried steak. It came with a crisp salad of lettuce, cabbage, carrots, and radishes on a dinner-sized plate. The chicken-fried steak was excellent. It was tender, and Jerry's special breading was flavorful. A small bowl of thick, country gravy was served on the side. The hashbrowns, a side of vegetables, and the chicken-fried steak covered the large plate. They were out of pie that night, dang it, so they served Debbie's chocolate truffles as a dessert with the meal. Debbie's right—you don't walk out of the Country Inn hungry.

Located twenty miles south of North Platte, the cafe makes one wonder how it could succeed in such an isolated location. Debbie concedes that it might be the food, but she admits it might also be because it's the only bathroom between North Platte and McCook. We agree with the customers who've asked Debbie if they could hook up to the Country Inn and haul it, good cooking and all, back to their hometowns.

Breakfast at the Tunnel Inn in Story, Wyoming

That first sweet movement into onion
tells us that the hashbrowns here
are created daily from scratch.

At my right hand
a chicken high on sacrifice
spreads itself yellow as yolk
across a white porcelain plate.

On the dance floor
the ghosts of last night's cowpoke couples
are liquid, too,
the boys in the band behind them
gone giddy with the low notes
of their own exhaustion.

With fingers crossed we toast a pledge
never to drink that much
Indiana rotgut bourbon whiskey ever again,
the black coffee an appropriate scalding
against the tongue.

Outside, where the morning
is girding its blue loins
with straps of cirrus,
a painted pony and a pickup
are dozing to the last strains of
Please release me.

Through an open door
fresh air with its stringtie
pink to the point of innocence
walks in. Hello, Big Guy.
Hello, bright light in each eye
at the end of each tunnel.

The last cowpoke couple
doffs its collective hat,
disappears like the ghost that it is
over a most promising
horizon.

—William Kloefkorn

West

Yellow Rose Cafe - Gering Nebraska

Oregon Trail Wagon Train

308-586-1850

Bayard

Gordon Howard and his family operate one of Nebraska's most unusual outdoor restaurants. It nestles in the shadows of one of Nebraska's greatest landmarks—Chimney Rock.

Howard is the grandson of a fur trader, and his family has lived on land adjacent to Chimney Rock for more than one hundred years. Thickly whiskered, tanned, and sturdily built, he has the look of a frontiersman, the strength and endurance of the wagon train boss, and the personality of an entertainer. There's some professor in him, too; he reveres the history of this area and enjoys sharing his extensive knowledge with his guests.

In addition to western-style cookouts in the summer, the family operation provides, by reservation only, living-history wagon treks lasting from three hours to six days. "We want people to understand how it really was, not how it is in the movies. It's pretty authentic, except for the chemical toilets. No use being miserable," Gordon says with a grin.

If you go for the chuck wagon steak dinner, held every day except Thursday during the summer, plan to arrive early so you can ride in a Conestoga wagon pulled by a team of mules for a close-up view of Chimney Rock. After the wagon ride, there is time for a beverage and a leisurely stroll along the Platte River or through the Howards' scenic grounds, once a favorite camping spot for wagon trains.

As chow time nears, hungry guests gather around the huge grill to enjoy the banter and bustle of the cooking crew as they adroitly grill thick, juicy rib eye steak—enough to feed a crowd. Served chuck wagon style, the meal also includes baked potatoes, relishes, creamed green beans, sourdough bread, and homemade ice cream. Patrons eat at rough lumber picnic tables set under a timber shelter. The food is plentiful and satisfying. A campfire and old-fashioned sing-along conclude the evening.

On summer Thursdays, the Howards serve an authentic pioneer menu: trail stew, hoecakes, spoon bread, relishes, sourdough bread, and vinegar pudding. In the winter the operation moves to a nearby cabin and serves prime rib by the light of lanterns and a huge fireplace.

An evening at the Oregon Trail Wagon Train is a family memory in the making. Every Nebraskan ought to enjoy it.

Sweet Things Bakery   *308-262-1024*
Bridgeport

When you approach Bridgeport from the east, traveling along the same route as pioneers in the mid-nineteenth century, you see rising to the south an immense bluff dwarfing a smaller bluff. Courthouse Rock and the smaller Jail Rock were the two landmarks on the trails west through Nebraska. Private Cornelius Conway of the Utah Expedition of 1857 wrote that "between Forts Kearny and Laramie the magnificent scenery is unsurpassed, probably unequalled in the world. From what is called Courthouse Rock by Chimney Rock, on to Scott's Bluff, there is an opacity in the mountains that is at once grand and sublime."

Courthouse Rock is well worth exploring. But before you do, explore the Sweet Things Bakery. Order a picnic lunch of bakery-fresh deli sandwiches, soups, and salads. Or if you want to be fancy as you explore, order a quiche.

Olde Main Street Inn
Chadron

115 Main St.
308-432-3380

The Olde Main Street Inn in Chadron is a saloon, pool hall, fine dining establishment, and hotel all rolled into one. In fact, three generations of strong women are pulling together in this old property to continue a thriving business.

The fascinating story starts with a determined mother, Eva Gore-Bracken, who leased a rough building to create a lounge to support herself and her family. In fits and starts, the place was returned to working order, and once she purchased the building in 1969, the renovation took off in earnest. Daughter Jeanne Goetzinger now runs the place, and with the help of her daughter, Lorri Pickrill, the old Chadron Hotel will soon be as fine as in the good old days. And frankly, it's probably a lot more fun today.

There's a lot going on in this place. Out front close to the street is a typical bar, but food is served there and the atmosphere is lively. Toward the back is a pool room, and if you continue walking down a few steps, you'll enter the "Cave" which has become a beautiful, fine dining room with rustic stone fireplace and fountain in the spot where the hotel's well was located. There are cozy corners for couples and lots of space for dancing and carrying-on.

The menu is varied, reasonably priced, and the family is proud that it offers more than just bar food. Naturally, there is a buffalo burger and buffalo steak and lots of beef. The Inn has lamb on the menu, smoked bratwurst, and chicken to name just a few items. Save room for a wonderful slice of Mud Pie, a family recipe that's unlike any other you've tried.

If you're road weary, you can rent sleeping rooms upstairs. A few have been completely restored; others are comfortable.

The Olde Main Street Inn is obviously a labor of love. This fine establishment is taking its rightful place as a social center in Chadron.

Bush's Gaslight
Gering

3315 No. 10th
308-632-7315

When we walked in, a lean westerner was wrestling with one of the biggest hunks of beef we've ever seen. "How much did that steak weigh before you started?" We asked. "They say it's twenty ounces. It's called the chunk," he said, while slicing off another juicy sliver.

We tried a junior variety of the chunk and were duly impressed. If you're in the Scottsbluff area and get a craving for steak, this is the place you should eat it.

Giggling Gourmet
Gering

1520 10th St.
308-436-5170

There's nothing funny about the food at the Giggling Gourmet. These are serious gourmet vittles. The first time we visited it was simply a gourmet take-out store. Now it's added eat-in luncheon selections. The food is unusual and tasty. There's soup of the day and salads served in edible bread bowls. Talk about variety—the bread bowls, which may be purchased for takeout, include Romano, Swiss & parsley, sour cream, or peasant. Sandwiches are served on New York-style bagels or homemade bread. Entrees include chicken or beef lasagna, turkey tetrazzini, beef shepherd's pie, chicken, beef or seafood stir-fry with bread, muffin or egg roll. Desserts range from low fat to decadent—fruit sorbet, apple dumplings, bread pudding, cheesecake, cinnamon ice cream, mud pie, chocolate mousse, and more. If you can't find something you like in the fare at the Giggling Gourmet, you can't be serious.

My Victorian Heart

Gering

1110 O St.
308-436-5080

Just as women have moved into grills formerly for "men-only," men are beginning to realize that tearoom fare ranks right up there with steak and beer. This quiet, unique tearoom serves excellent gourmet lunches. Fresh flowers on the table and classical music for background make this a classy place with unusual dishes. It serves excellent soups, salads and desserts. A western oasis of food carefully prepared by women who love to cook, it's popular with the ladies who lunch crowd, but men should try it.

Sioux Sundries

Harrison

308-668-2577

Sioux Sundries, a modest-looking building from the outside, has a guest book with signatures from all fifty states and fourteen foreign countries. For an eatery in a town of 360, far from major population centers, that's quite an accomplishment. Plaques on the wall include the state tourism award and the Beef Backer Award from the Nebraska Beef Board. Sioux Sundries has been mentioned in *USA Today*, *Stars and Stripes*, and other publications, and it was featured by Charles Kuralt on CBS' *Sunday Morning*.

What brings them in? Oddly, the little nondescript store-front lunch counter is home to one of the biggest hamburgers on the planet—the famous Coffee burger. Named for a local rancher who wanted to feed his hands in a big way, the twenty-eight-ounce burger gets raves, but no one's ever asked for seconds. It's an amazing sandwich, perched precariously on a normal-sized bun. It comes with the usual accompaniments and the odd bag of cholesterol-free chips. Natch.

Located on a corner of the main street, Sioux Sundries doesn't look like a restaurant. It isn't. It's a store where you can buy toothpaste, shampoo, bag balm, duct tape, kitchen knives, toys, graduation presents, diapers, photo albums, key rings, magazines, rain bonnets, videos, romance novels (new and used), and short-order meals. It's an antique Stop-and-Shop. If they don't have it, you don't need it.

The food can be found at the back in a tiny space large enough for five booths and a chrome-and-Formica lunch counter.

The Coffee burger was excellent—well-seasoned, flavorful, and not greasy. We asked the waitress the secret of the burgers. She claimed it was the freshness of the meat and admitted the size may add some novelty. "There may be a bigger burger somewhere," she said, "but until we find it, we're going to bill it as the world's largest." In our culinary travels, we've found nothing to dispute her claim.

Carol's Cafe   308-487-3422
Hemingford

It was ninety-nine degrees on an August afternoon when we rolled into Hemingford hunting for Carol's Cafe. Huge grain trucks, five blocks deep, filled main street waiting in line to dump their wheat at the elevator on the north side of downtown. The drivers, ranging in age from sixteen to eighty, were mostly sitting in the shade trading stories or drinking pop. But we were looking to load up and had heard that Carol's Cafe was *the* place in Hemingford.

Carol's is an unself-conscious icon of small-town America. Squeaky clean, showing the touch of a woman who wants things just so, the cafe offers tidy tables that overlook main street. The customers talk about land prices, cattle, and wheat. If it has a back room, the Rotary Club probably meets there. Along the walls are an unusual collection of caricatures of local residents and national figures. Tom Osborne is the only one in color. The chicken-fried steak and chicken and noodles represent the best of basic country cooking— good quality and plenty of it. Also try Carol's stuffed potatoes. They're a highlight in the heart of wheat country.

Mi Ranchito   *308-235-4498*
Kimball

Our favorite Panhandle Mexican cafe has moved from Scottsbluff to open anew in Kimball.

We love tamales, and Mi Ranchito makes great tamales. Homemade ones. Ai-yai-yai! Prepared with a coating of grainy cornmeal—almost a thick, chewy hide—surrounding shredded, seasoned beef and smothered with a choice of red or green chile. They are superb! You'll want to load a cooler with a batch to bring home. There are other traditional items and a wide variety of Mexican breakfast dishes like huevos rancheros and huevos Mexicana (eggs mixed with jalapenos, onions, tomatoes, beans, and a tortilla). We also sampled the huevos chorizo (Mexican sausage).

The interior arches, pillars, beams, white walls, and Mexican music give Mi Ranchito a south-of-the-border feel. A large mural of a Mexican beach near the back and, of course, sombreros and serapes on the walls of the renovated building add to the atmosphere.

The family staff is friendly and truly appreciates hearing your compliments. When we rave about the tamales, they always proudly say, "We make our own."

The burro dessert is unique, a burrito with fruit inside and a scoop of ice cream on top. It cools the fire left from the spicy entrees.

Cattlemen's   308-762-8347
Lakeside

Several years ago we had one of the best steaks ever at the Cattlemen's. Started by ranchers in the area, it closed for awhile. Now it's sprung to life again and worth a try. Typical steakhouse fare.

Vic's Steakhouse and Lounge   308-778-5801
Lewellen

Nebraskans are meat eaters. We've located only two vegetarian restaurants in Nebraska, one in Omaha, and one in the small town of Milford. That was last summer; now there's only one.

No, Nebraskans will never be vegetarians. We're tolerant people: we'll accept the fact that someone gambles, drinks, cusses, chews 'n' spits, and hates to shave and take baths, but a vegetarian is as strange as someone who doesn't root for Big Red. Perhaps being a vegetarian is healthy. We agree, however, with Calvin Trillin who says, "Healthy food makes me sick." Furthermore, meat can't be too bad for us. A recent health survey ranked Nebraska ninth in overall health.

Which brings us, finally, to Vic's Steakhouse. It serves great steaks. And for the vegetarian in you, the salad bar ain't bad either.

The Roost   308-772-3552
Lisco

It's a long stretch from Ogallala to Scottsbluff. We're usually starved by the time we hit Lisco, so we stop for lunch at the only cafe in town. Formerly known as the C Bar T and Custer's Last Stand, it's recently become the Roost. When it was Custer's, two Lincoln friends, Bruce Wright and Mike McNair, who have healthy appetites to go with substantial silhouettes, strongly recommended this place. The good news is that the cook who now rules the Roost used to work at Custer's.

We've haven't yet been to The Roost. But we have great faith in the fine tastes of these two gentlemen. If they say the cook can cook; he can cook. And besides, with their size, who are we to argue?

The Flame   308-783-1727
Melbeta

Like moths to flame, folks in the Panhandle flock to a special restaurant in Melbeta. The steakhouse that draws them in is rightly named the Flame. You want abalone, smoked octopus, escargot, frog legs, oysters, quail, or trout along with your steak? Then this is the place! The amazing variety of good food at the Flame confounds the "location, location, location" chant recited by the business experts. The theme at the Flame is "juicy steaks, juicy steaks, juicy steaks" and it keeps pulling 'em in.

Dude's Steak House
Sidney

2126 Illinois
308-254-9080

Among family members, Dick is regarded as The Condiment King. He's known to slather catsup, mustard, and steak sauce on food with the restraint of a brick mason slapping on mortar. And we may have the only refrigerator in Seward County with four opened bottles of chutney, several steak sauces, two wee bottles of unearthly hot Tiger Sauce (the size belies its power), and a wide range of variations on the catsup theme, from basil to barbecue. And that doesn't count the mustards.

Dick's affinity for condiments is well known. One friend reminds him that he doesn't need to use condiments. "That's easy for you to say," Dick retorts, "but four kids are enough!"

Naturally, The Condiment King is attracted to places that feature a full array of condiments, especially if a novel steak sauce is a specialty of the house. That's what attracted him to Dude's, where Country Bob Edson's All-Purpose Steak Sauce is featured. It's sweet and spicy, flavored with vinegar, anchovies, and Worcestershire. Just the thing a condiment connoisseur likes to tie into. And Dude's Steakhouse has an enormous variety of dishes—eleven kinds of steak plus barbecue, rabbit, chicken, and pheasant—to smother.

We had the filet. We knew it would be good even before tasting it. We knew it from the fine grilled aroma that wafted across the table and announced this is a great piece of meat. One of us ate it without sauce. One of us had filet au Country Bob.

We're not decorators, but a western theme permeates the establishment. The bar alongside is the Branding Iron, and the prints on the wall are exclusively western—individually lit, no less.

Dude's draws a good crowd most nights and opens for breakfast at 5:30 a.m. It's in downtown Sidney, an example of how you can find good eats if you're willing to eschew I-80 fast food and venture into the towns that line the Interstate.

Sanna's
Sidney

917 Illinois St.
308-254-4013

Things come slowly to Nebraska. New ideas seem to start on the coasts, inching their way toward Nebraska until they overwhelm us with their novelty and then seem commonplace. This is true whether it's fashion, body piercing, skateboarding, tattoos, hiking-biking trails, cowboy line dancing, or cappuccino. Who'da thunk it? A classy cappuccino parlor not in Sacramento, not in Sarasota, but in Sidney. And its immodest name reveals expansive vision. This is not your neighborhood coffee shop. This is Sanna's Cappuccino International.

There are advantages to being slow in making cultural advances. We let the rest of the country work out the kinks of new notions, and when they're through tinkering, we finally decide to do it. And at this point we can do it right. That's what Sanna's does. It offers a wide variety of gourmet coffees—and does it as well as they do anywhere on the coasts. And what's more, there's another discovery sweeping across the Nebraska plains—bagels. They have them, too, at Sanna's. In fact they serve them not only for breakfast, but also as deli sandwiches at lunch. Things are getting downright progressive in the Nebraska cafes (the next thing Nebraska restaurants will discover is that there's more than one kind of lettuce.)

But seriously, Sanna's is neat. Melody Sanna has created a cappuccino parlor out of an historic old building which was once an upstairs hotel for railroad men, the kind of men who preferred strong coffee. They'd have ordered Sanna's espresso. The building has big front windows, high ceilings, canopies, umbrellas, old wooden ladder chairs, and fancy tablecloths. The decor is creative, the coffee first class, and the sandwiches memorable. Spend some time at Sanna's.

El Charrito
Scottsbluff

802 21st Ave.
308-632-3534

El Charrito is short on decor and long on flavor. A perennial Mexican favorite in Scottsbluff, El Charrito has the ambience of an Army mess hall; even the hats and serapes are missing. There are no waitresses and a radio blares rock and roll or country western instead of mariachi serenades. You stand in line to place your order, then take it away from the window when it's ready.

Order anything with green chile. Our meal was three-alarm hot with chunks of pork and green chilies. The milder guacamole, a tasty blend of fresh avocado, lemon juice, and garlic, helped cool down the chile. Reportedly, El Charrito is a favorite western haunt of Senator Bob Kerrey.

Rosita's

Scottsbluff

1205 E. Orchard
308-632-2429

How can you tell a good Mexican restaurant? We use a few signs to tip us off to winners. First we examine the classic starters: margaritas, chips, and salsa are indicators of what's to come. Many times you can rate the place based on these first few tastes. Rosita's, our favorite in a covey of good Mexican cantinas in Scottsbluff, always passes this test. The chips are unique. Fried, of course, they are puffy, layered, always fresh and warm, almost like good puff pastry. They're strikingly different from the versions offered at other Mexican eateries. The salsa is a bright note—fresh, chunky, tomatoey, and just spicy enough with traces of cilantro. It passed the scrutiny of a tough grader, Broken Bow salsa expert Kerri Lewandowski, a dinner companion on our last visit.

The margaritas are the right stuff. Big and chilly, they strike a nice balance between sweet and sour. With Rosita's guacamole, thick with big chunks of seasoned avocado, margaritas are a perfect accompaniment.

Rosita's has contemporary decor. White and red dominate the color scheme. Sombreros, parrots, and red peppers are sprinkled throughout. Whimsical red pepper blades on the ceiling fans waft soft breezes. You'll think you're sitting in a Mexican cantina.

The corn tacos are made with the same fried, puffy dough as the chips. We had chicken smothered with fresh lettuce and tomato. Flour tacos are available, too. A full array of tasty dishes, including burritos, enchiladas, and chiles relleno, are listed on the menu. The service is friendly and fast.

137

From the very first chip, Rosita's is good. In fact, Rosita's shares many of the attributes of a good tortilla chip. It's inexpensive, its flavor exceeds its appearance, and it'll keep you coming back for more. Rosita's is one of the best Mexican choices in Nebraska.

The Woodshed

Scottsbluff

18 East 16th
308-635-3684

Most Nebraskans dread going to the woodshed, but being sent to the Woodshed in Scottsbluff is a treat. The patrons who enjoy this eatery are not gluttons for *punishment*, but they're gluttons just the same, and you can count us among them.

The fare is East Coast eclectic. The owners came from the East to teach at now-defunct Hiram Scott College, loved the West, and took root. The fare at the Woodshed is a potpourri of big-city flavors. If New York deli is your mood, there's the hot pastrami on rye. If it's Italian, there's pasta. And if you feel like polishing off a Polish dish, go on Thursday, Friday, or Saturday for the Woodshed specialty—Polish pierogis, dumplings filled with cabbage. None other than food goddess Martha Stewart loves pierogis, claiming, "I have consumed up to twenty of these delectable dumplings at one sitting." Really, Martha? You won't be able to finish twenty, but the pierogis are worth a try. The next time we go back, there'll probably be something even more exotic on the menu, and we can't wait to find out what it might be.

"Two a.m. in the Village Inn, alone, in tears, my notebook
under my arm, the waitress brought me toast, shook her head
under her hairnet and said, 'Honey, it'll get worse before
it gets better. Drink up this hot coffee.'
In the lot under the streetlight the Rambler station wagon sat in two feet of snow
and O Street was emptied of everyone over sixteen."

—from "Lincoln" by Hilda Raz

Lincoln

The Tastee Inn - Lincoln, Ne.

If you're starstruck, dreaming of a career in the theater, then strolling through the stage-door entrance to Barrymore's Lounge is a dream come true. At Barrymore's you can tread the boards where theater legends have walked. Here in the alley between O and P streets, next to the Stuart Building, is a door to the past—backstage at the once elegant Stuart Theater.

The entrance to Barrymore's is the original stage door, the same door used by Helen Hayes and Mickey Rooney in the heyday of the Stuart Theater. As you enter, the light board/control panel on your left is complete with all the backstage technical equipment. The long ropes on the right controlled the battens and backdrops now hoisted high over your head. Look up. The vast open area extends 110 feet, that's more than ten stories to the ceiling. The lounge itself is located right on the stage, the back of the bar is right behind the screen of the still operating movie theater.

The stars' dressing rooms on the west side of the second floor are now restrooms. They're all original except for carpet and paint. The chorus' dressing rooms on the second and third floors at the east end are now meeting rooms.

Musicians entered the orchestra pit in the basement directly below your seats. The individual lights over each table, which create an intimate atmosphere, were created from the footlights at the edge of the pit. The conductor's podium now holds hors d'oeuvres.

Although space allows only a very small kitchen, the sandwiches are excellent. They are appropriately named the Bogart, Groucho, Garbo, and all, and there's a low-cal one named after the owner, Jim Haberlan, who is on a perpetual diet. The Grant sandwich is the specialty of the house. It's a combination of cream cheese, onions, walnuts, black olives, lemon juice, and sliced turkey.

A unique item on the menu is historic Lebsack's Chili. This dish closely resembles the tasty but grease-laden chili served by the Lebsack brothers about a block from the present-day Barrymore's. If you were around Lincoln in the '50s and '60s, you'll remember it.

Barrymore's was opened in 1974 by Haberlan, a Lincoln architect with a theatrical bent and a commitment to historic preservation. He has created a one-of-a-kind place to have a drink, enjoy quiet conversation, or simply sit back and listen to some of the best bar music around (from jazz to classical). With an atmosphere like that, it's easy to dream of being a star.

Billy's
Lincoln

1301 H Street
402-474-0084

Billy's is a stone's throw from the State Capitol, the watering hole of choice for the staffers, pols, officials, and lobbyists who haunt the Statehouse. The business of governing is conducted at noon and continues after hours at Billy's, a restaurant located in a tastefully restored home with a beautiful, new exterior paint job.

Nebraska political memorabilia make up the decoration; don't come expecting the frosting and gingerbread of a Victorian mansion. This is a plain, but attractive dining room where food and conversation are the focus; while you're waiting, check out the fascinating items. The restaurant has had the same skilled chef since its opening. He creates an interesting variety of dishes. Lunch is a good time to try the specials. They're usually served quickly and are priced moderately. Visit the bar after work to view the who's who of political life in the state.

The restaurant is irreverently named for Lincoln's illustrious William Jennings Bryan, three-time U. S. presidential nominee and a lifelong teetotaler. We wonder what Bryan would have thought of this restaurant named in his honor. Somehow we think he would have enjoyed himself here.

Blue Heron Wine Bar and Bistro
Lincoln

555 So. 48th Street
402-421-9555

The Blue Heron is off the beaten track, and it's easy for us to overlook. When we visit, which is not often enough, we always wonder why we don't go there more often. This place has a gift for hospitality. It's casual, yet upscale with tremendous food and a very fine wine list, as you can imagine with Ken Meier at the helm. In fact, first time patrons may think they've wandered into a wine shop because the bistro is located away from the front door. Walk back and step down into a vineyard with vines twining overhead in an inviting fashion. Fine food and wine is the focus here.

We like the variety of the entrees and the emphasis on seasonal produce. There are many dishes to try that you might not find anywhere else. We also enjoy the fact that menu includes both sandwiches and salads and full meals so everyone can be satisfied. Another draw for us is that they use wonderful fresh herbs from a grower near Beatrice; it makes a flavorful difference.

For unusual entrees served with a selection of excellent wines, the Blue Heron may be Lincoln's best restaurant.

The Cookie Company

Lincoln

138 No. 12th

402-475-0625

Every noon Dick trudges to the YMCA to exercise. He runs, he bends, he twists, he strains, he sweats, and when he's finished, he's famished. Hoping to keep the pounds off, he tries to skip lunch. But Cookie Company owner Elizabeth Wanamaker will have none of it. He says she intentionally selected the site between his office and the YMCA, knowing he'd walk by hungry each day. He complains that if seeing the cookies in the window is not enough, and if knowing what's inside is not enough, Elizabeth went so far as to install a so-called ventilation fan. He calls it her cookie seduction device, and claims it's a secret weapon designed to spew the alluring aroma of fresh-baked cookies into his face. He says this diabolical machine has the same purpose as a beautiful woman's perfume.

Elizabeth's strategy works. Instead of skipping lunch, or being content with something light—a broth soup or a salad with low cal dressing—Dick stops at the Cookie Company almost every day. His intentions are good: "I'll have only the raisin oatmeal. Raisins are fruit; oats are high protein." But, alas, this logic can be stretched. And he stretches it—all the

way to chocolate, peanut butter, macadamia nut, and snick-
erdoodle. He says you never know when a natural disaster
will force you to stay in your office for days, and only those
with adequate food will survive.

These are Nebraska's best cookies. No wonder Dick can't
resist buying one, or two, or three, or a full sack.

The Cornhusker Hotel   *333 So. 13th*
Terrace Grille/The Renaissance   *402-474-7474*
Lincoln

Years ago, Nebraskans visiting the Capital City enjoyed
special events at The Cornhusker. The Tee Pee Room and
Pow Wow Room were gathering places before and after NU
games, big dates, and other significant events in the city.
People fondly remember some of their favorite items on the
old menus and enjoy recalling good times spent at The
Cornhusker. These days the venerable Cornhusker is trying
to create a new set of memories.

The Terrace Grille, the former coffee shop on the first floor,
got a face-lift recently along with a new menu, and it seems
to attract a pretty steady crowd. There are creative, unusual
items on the menu; old standbys like chicken Caesar salad
and a Reuben sandwich; and interesting pastas and lighter
entrees that seem to take advantage of more fresh, natural
ingredients. Besides the revamped menu, you've got to see
the place to believe it. The Cornhusker spent a pretty penny
creating a one-of-a-kind atmosphere with elaborate, painted
effects. Garden landscapes grace every wall, creating three-
dimensional dioramas in the tiny spaces for dining. The
murals, painted by a California artist, depict, with a little
artistic license, the famous gardens of the world. It's a
sensational look, and depending where you sit, the room

may look entirely different each time you visit. Breakfast, lunch, and dinner are served here with different menus at each meal.

The Renaissance is still *the* formal dining spot in Lincoln. It has starched linens, quiet service, and candlelight. Big windows look out at the passing scene. The night-lit State Capitol is a lovely backdrop to special events. The staff will make a fuss over you on special occasions, and many entrees can be cooked tableside. Big dates, big life events deserve The Renaissance.

With these two new landmarks anchoring The Cornhusker, folks fifty years from now will also have fond memories to recall.

Crane River   *200 No. 11th*
Lincoln   *402-476-7766*

Another popular brew-pub is Crane River, located just one block south of the Lied Center at 11th and P streets. This is a bright, airy spot with big windows looking out onto the sidewalk so you can watch passersby. There are also a few tables set up outside to enjoy mild weather.

Like all micro-breweries, Crane River has its brewery set up so patrons can see the action. Large copper and stainless steel kettles and pipes are arranged behind glass walls. The brewer's art is good here. We like the whooping wheat beer, a wheat-based brew served with a lemon slice, and the pivo, a nod to Nebraska's Czech heritage, but there are several others to try.

When we want a hearty snack or a simple meal before a movie in Lincoln, we will order the Crane River artichoke dip to share and two cups of the yummy tomato-dill soup, which is out of this world. The soup is a creamy-style tomato with delicious herbs. It really has a fresh-from-the-garden taste, and it's a special treat on a freezing winter day.

This eatery has quite an unusual menu. You'll find many items that can't be found anywhere else, such as venison and elk. There are buffalo burgers, too. But don't be put off by the novelty fare. There are familiar, comforting dishes, as well.

When you visit, be sure to notice the long, wall-sized quilt hanging on the north side of the bar area. This beautiful work of art, made locally, depicts the annual sandhill crane migration, hence the name of the restaurant, Crane River.

Dem Bonz   *4640 Bair Ave.*
Lincoln   *402-477-3340*

Several years ago we made a barbecue tour of southern Georgia. We drove and we ate. We traveled from Soperton to Statesboro, from Hapeville to Valdosta. We feasted at Sweat's, Zeb's, The Flying Pig, the Ga. Pig, and the Home Folk's Corner. We sampled real barbecue—that mystical blend of fire, smoke, meat, and sauce. Yes, real barbecue, barbecue that satisfies a ravenous appetite and takes only twenty minutes, eight napkins, and a splattered shirt to devour. Real barbecue, consumed with simplicity—on paper plates with plastic tableware and spongy white bread to soak up the juice. Georgia is real barbecue paradise; the kind of barbecue that we Nebraskans have only been able to dream about.

But there's hope. Dem Bonz has arrived. And it brings to our great state the kind of real barbecue that experts Greg

Johnson and Vince Staten have described in *Food and Wine* as "so meltingly tender and suffused with flavor that mere mortals ought to thank their lucky Wet Naps that the gods didn't keep it to themselves."

As we walked into Dem Bonz, the scent of smoke and sauce brought back thoughts of Georgia. There was plenty to choose from. Dem Bonz has everything from chicken to brisket sandwiches to baby back ribs. Gluttony strikes— you'll find yourself reaching for another rib before you've completed the one you're working on. The meat: moist and tender, cooked to perfection with a smoky flavor and no burnt char to speak of. The sauce: secret, of course, and distinctive, blending something sweet, vinegary, with to-mato and a tinge of heat. Once the first bite of 'que crosses your lips and the earthy flavor and hickory smoke seep into your bloodstream, you're hooked.

The sides are also noteworthy. There's Mrs. Freeman's (a family friend) tangy cole slaw and potato salad—right up there with the best you've eaten at a potluck picnic. The baked beans, quite sweet, seem laced with molasses. The corn bread may be better than Grandma's. It's moist and buttery, not the dry version that sticks in your craw. And finally, there's the all-time favorite southern dessert, sweet potato pie. It's like finding the Holy Grail.

Dem Bonz is the creation of Carey Pettigrew and Dennis Cornett-Ang. They know what they're doing. Located in far north Lincoln, its interior is bright and spotless. What it lacks in charm, it makes up for in hygiene when compared with the places in Georgia. Dem Bonz has the food to meet the real barbecue test. You'll walk out with a big old sauce-eatin' grin on your face.

El Mercadito Mexican Market

Lincoln

1028 O
402-435-6774

We don't normally select eateries based on portion size alone, but in the case of El Mercadito, we have to make an exception. This downtown take-out market serves the most substantial burritos of any available in Lincoln. Come here for one-pound burritos—we're not kidding, we've weighed them. You'd better bring help, if you're carrying back lunch for a crowd!

Even if this Mexican market served puny, four-ounce burritos, we'd recommend them because they are delicious and, quite frankly, we think they may be the best in the world.

Located on the north side of O Street between 10th and 11th, the business is finally catching on, according to owners Norma and Ray Torrejon. It's about time.

The deli case is right inside the front door. Order a ten-inch or twelve-inch burrito, the size depends on the diameter of the flour tortilla. We usually get one twelve-inch to share between two people.

The tortillas are packed with a bean and rice combination, chicken, some lettuce, and chile of your choice. We always pick chile verde—the green variety. It has a little fire and lots of flavor. Just the right amount of cilantro, for example.

There are tacos, too; roasted chicken and skirt steak are available for carnivores. You can also order a marinated steak to take home to grill. Known as carne para azar, it is marinated in his own special mixture, Ray explains with pride. You can order it by the pound to take home for the weekend.

Ray is also hoping to attract the football crowd. He wants his gigantic burritos to be the food of choice for fans heading to the stadium. We say that's a great idea, and hope it catches on.

The Four Suns
Lincoln

2901 NW 48th St.
402-470-2003

"Sawadee ka." Daughter Laura greeted Pimpa Mills, the owner of the Four Suns Cafe, an austere Thai restaurant in an unlikely location west of Air Park in Lincoln. Laura spent two years in Thailand, and not only speaks Thai, but claims to know good, authentic Thai food. We have introduced her to several other Thai restaurants in the Lincoln area, but the food from the Four Suns is the first she describes as really authentic.

The authenticity is the result of the one-woman kitchen skills of Pimpa, who grew up in rural Thailand; she's a friendly woman with the trademark Thai smile.

We gave Laura carte blanche to order what she thought we'd like. She insisted on one of her Thai favorites, som tom, a green papaya salad. It tastes a little like Korean kim chee: it has a strong cabbage taste, fermentation a step past sauerkraut, combined with chili peppers, lime juice, and garlic. It's a combination that takes some adjustment for Americans, but after hearing Laura's sighs of delight on countless occasions, we keep trying it. And we must admit, we're getting to like it—some. We also had larb gai salad, which Laura says is really a Laotian dish adopted by the Thais. Try it, you'll add Laotian to your repertoire. It has ground meat (your choice), fish sauce, peppers, garlic, and lots of cabbage.

We're big on soup, so we tried the tomkakai soup, and found it delicious. This is a mild-mannered soup with a surprising explosion of flavor. Coconut is the base of the taste sensation, but it's effused with citrusy vegetation—lemon grass, lime leaves and galanga root.

We rode the Thai roller coaster further with pad thai, a Thai standard that wasn't as satisfying (more peanut, please), and finished with a powerful green curry chicken entree, geng keoh wan. It was quite *pet* (spicy) and required an extra glass of *nam* (water) to cool our tongues, but it was very good with lots of rice.

Go to the Four Suns for food, not atmosphere. There is a small dining room, but most people take out. And don't be in a hurry. Remember that Pimpa is a one-woman show, racing around the open kitchen like a sailor handing out life jackets to passengers on a sinking ship. Her cooking has attracted a steady increase in customers, and she struggles to keep up with the demand. As we left, Laura complimented Pimpa. "Kap koon ka." (Thank you.) "Aroy!" (Delicious!)

Garden Cafe   *70th & A*
Lincoln   *402-434-3750*

See Omaha listing.

Green Gateau   *330 So. 10th*
Lincoln   *402-477-0330*

The Green Gateau is a spot of jolly old England plunked down just a block from Lincoln's County-City building. This is a tiny cafe that seems to fill a special niche in the Capital City.

From a culinary perspective, it always seems to please. First, it serves an early morning breakfast that's hearty and always delicious. It has wonderful coffees and teas in addition to pastries. Egg dishes, old-world oatmeal, and granola will certainly get your day off to a good start. The luncheon fare is popular—usually soups, salads, and sandwiches that are far from run-of-the-mill. Dinners are also well prepared, and there's a resplendent dessert menu for late evening enjoyment or as an accompaniment to a meal. One tempting feature is an enormous country-style dinner roll, a delicious addition to most salads, soups, and entrees. In fact, a bowl of soup with a roll could easily make a meal.

One of the most attractive features of this cozy hideaway is its resemblance to a tiny, neighborhood teahouse in England. The linens and china are mismatched. English bric-a-brac are strewn about, and there's dark, English, oak furniture of indeterminate vintage. Lovely, dark paneling adds to the warmth of the rooms, and enhances an interesting stained glass window set into the ceiling in the center of the restaurant. Despite its gentle ambience, the Green Gateau serves portions hearty enough to appeal to a big eater. Men seem to love the food, and everyone appreciates the quiet, good taste of the atmosphere and the fine service. The Green Gateau might be a hit with nearly everyone. We feel lucky to have it close at hand.

Grottos
Lincoln

1100 O Street
402-475-9475

Grottos has evolved from the Lincoln landmark, The Rotisserie. They've adopted a brighter, lighter look with the feel of casual dining. The food is just as good, and the prices are lower to reflect the more casual atmosphere. Some Lincolnites still mourn the passing of the old-style Rotisserie with its white linens and soothing atmosphere, but now many new people have taken to this upbeat place with the colorful, contemporary decor.

We usually head to the cellar to spend time with Herb Thomas who is the greatest host in North America. He remembers our favorite beverages and plays the finest music available, while juggling a dozen tables. He teaches customers about wine, food, and music, and holds his own in discussions of contemporary literature or political intrigue.

The brochettes are tops in terms of entrees with your choice of side dishes to accompany the meat selection. We've been pleased with the turkey tandoori. The pastas are also delicious. You can order smaller portions of nearly everything on the menu which adds to the flexibility.

Grottos is the centerpiece now for Lincoln's lively cafe society.

Imperial Palace
Lincoln

707 North 27th
402-474-2688

Stanley Jou, owner of the Imperial Palace, says he knows the names of 1,500 customers. The last time we were there he was able to tell us (correctly) the number of years we'd been regulars. During that period of time, we've had attentive service, excellent meals, and the delight of being personally greeted by our first names every time we enter the establishment.

This smooth operation is a marvel, and it could be a lesson to other restaurateurs. Staff turnover seems minimal, and no matter who serves the meal, friendly, cheerful, and skillful help is at hand.

The interior evokes Chinese themes. The main dining room is tasteful and appropriate to the cuisine; lots of red, black lacquer, and gold trim predominate. A pretty, new dining room has been added in the back. It has a more contemporary look, with big windows and light walls with fewer Chinese accessories. Throughout the restaurant, the atmosphere is informal, family-oriented and sometimes a little noisy, but the bustle seems comfortable.

The service is extraordinary, highlighted by personal attention: Stanley greets you by name at the door, the hostess shows you to your table, someone promptly fills your water glasses, the smiling server fills your teacups and takes your order, and the kitchen responds quickly.

The problem will be choosing from the expansive menu. For regular customers, Stanley also serves authentic dishes not listed on the menu. An interpreter is recommended, however, for an-off-the-menu eating odyssey.

Inn Harm's Way
Lincoln

201 No. 7th
402-438-3033

When Inn Harm's Way opened in the Lincoln Station several years ago, we were disappointed with it. However, we think it's Lincoln's most-improved restaurant. The service is excellent, the wine list is extensive, and the food, especially the seafood, is superb. Give it another try; you'll be pleased.

JaBrisco
Lincoln

700 P Street
402-474-7272

This is a casual dining destination. It's brought to you by the same fine folks who developed the brew-pub, Lazlo's, right next door. You can't beat this place for service and creativity.

Everyone is well trained to take care of diners. It's just that the atmosphere can drive you to distraction. It's a noisy, chaotic place, which may be part of its charm for some, but for people with chaotic lives, a simpler pace might be more enjoyable.

The folks at JaBrisco are trying all the latest restaurant trends: the open kitchen, wood-fired oven, eclectic decor, creative combination of ingredients in familiar food—pasta, pizza, salads. It gets everything right, and you certainly ought to try it for yourself to see how comfortable you feel.

The clever food is matched by a clever decor. It has a soft, industrial look with duct work visible and a spatter-painted ceiling. There are colorful accents on a darker background— mauve, blue, turquoise, purple, pink, and terra cotta. The place has a cosmopolitan menu and a wild look, but the food and service are top-notch.

Sit in the booths by the windows just south of the kitchen for the best soundproofing and most comfortable surroundings. There's no question that JaBrisco will feed you well, but you won't want to linger. Which, when we think about it, may be the whole idea. Hmmmmmm.

K's Restaurant

Lincoln

1275 So. Cotner
402-483-2858

K's has a new owner, but it's just as good as ever. It's a remarkably comfortable place with a fireplace, carpeting, wooden booths, dark paneling, and country antiques. And the food is comforting, too. The breakfasts are among the best in Lincoln. There are lots of interesting egg dishes; the Big Red omelette with ham, bacon, and Canadian bacon is as devastating as the Big Red offense. There are Belgian waffles and a to-kill-for pecan struedel coffee cake. There are great salads and sandwiches, and the dinners are excellent. The last time we visited, we had a terrific smoked pork chop served with a huge mound of mashed potatoes, gravy, and veggies.

For you movie buffs, scenes in *Terms of Endearment*, with Shirley McLaine and Jack Nicholson were filmed near the front window in the north dining room.

Lazlo's
Lincoln

710 P
402-474-2337

Lazlo's is an institution in Lincoln's Haymarket area. If you see crowds congregating on the sidewalk on P Street, they're probably waiting for a table at Lazlo's. This was Nebraska's first brew-pub, a hybrid tavern and brewery. With an on-premises brewery behind glass walls, Lazlo's was a curiosity early on. The novelty home brew was good, but the crowds came back for the great food and service, as well as the beer. An institution was born. The interesting thing about Lazlo's is that it seems to appeal to all ages. You'll see college students and retired couples; women friends celebrating next to guys out hoisting a few.

Although this eatery gets busy, the kitchen and wait staff seem to be able to handle nearly anything that comes up. They have some of the most consistent service of any restaurant in Nebraska. They train their servers to please and the crew goes out of its way to accommodate diners. If you don't like something, they'll make it right. The menu is elaborate sandwich fare with good soups and enormous main-course salads. The appetizers are plentiful—lavosh, a flat, crackerlike bread with toppings, is a perennial favorite. They serve a variety of entrees so everyone in your party can find something to enjoy.

The restaurant has added new dining rooms; upstairs to the west is space for quite a few people, and many nonsmokers enjoy the back room upstairs. It may seem to take awhile to get to your table, but the lines move quickly, and we think it's definitely worth the wait.

The Mill
Lincoln

800 P Street
402-475-5522

In the Haymarket area of Lincoln you can smell the delicious aroma of roasting coffee. If you follow your nose, you'll wind up at The Mill, Lincoln's premier coffeehouse. For a long time, The Mill owned the only coffee roaster between Chicago and Denver. There may be more than that now, but in Lincoln, the only coffee roaster in town can be found at The Mill, and that's what draws the Haymarket crowds who gather here in droves to enjoy the freshest, most aromatic coffee available. The roaster is a massive machine sitting just inside the front door next to a small bunch of tables. One of the owners, Dale Nordyke, will explain the roasting process—the temperature required for various beans, the time involved, and where the beans come from. It's a fascinating process. After roasting, the beans are ground into wonderful coffees. This is the place to try all the coffee drinks you've heard about: cappuccino, espresso, latte, mocha. There are a few snacks and some delicious, cold beverages, too.

The Mill is a coffee bar, small-town cafe, study hall for students and profs, meeting spot, and destination for the evening. At some point or another, everyone who works in a six-block radius will show up at The Mill for their cup of coffee and conversation.

Misty's
Lincoln

North: 6235 Havelock / 402-466-8424
South: 5508 So. 56th / 402-423-2288

Remember, this is the legendary Misty's Restaurant in Havelock, U. S. A., a reluctant annex of the city of Lincoln. This is the home of great prime rib served with heaping amounts of football memorabilia. For years thousands of Cornhusker fans have lined up to eat here after Saturday afternoons in Memorial Stadium. And for the truly crazed Husker fan, this is the place to visit in the off-season, as well. Don't say we didn't warn you.

While waiting for tables, fans study display cases filled with trophies, jerseys, photos, autographed footballs, and battle-scarred helmets. There's a football-shaped bar and a life-sized quarterback passing a ball in the direction of the cashier, an inspiring sight for fans who hunger for a passing game along with their steak. True fans will imagine the crashing of shoulder pads and the roar of the crowd until the perfume of grilling steaks brings Joe Husker back to the business at hand—tying into some top-ranked Nebraska beef.

No, don't expect quiche or cobb salad at Misty's. This is a shrine to the Huskers—that means football and beef. The star recruit is the prime rib, thick, tender, full of corn-fed flavor. For triple-threat taste, try the sizzling sirloin steak. It's thick, oozing with juices pink to slightly red, a real hunk of flavor. Even the burgers show up the competition.

There's a paler, upscale Misty's annex in south Lincoln designed for lazy suburban types who won't make the long trek up north. The food's the same, minus the Husker atmosphere.

When you walk out of Misty's, you'll have the same satisfied feeling of Husker fans after yet another national championship. How do you top that?

160

Molan's Bakery and Delicatessen

1244 South Street

Lincoln

402-434-2666

Molan's is Lincoln's premier bakery and deli. Melissa Spangler creates wonderful baked goods and pastries for many of Lincoln's best restaurants. We figure you might as well buy them, too. Her baguettes are scrumptious and as close to good French bread as you can get in Lincoln. She has sandwiches and salads to go, and magnificent desserts for special occasions. What's more, she caters! Located next to Meier's Cork and Bottle, Molan's is a good place to drive by on the way home.

The Oven

201 North 8th

Lincoln

402-475-6118

We love going to Lincoln's Haymarket, and one of the nicest spots in the neighborhood is The Oven, an Indian bistro in sophisticated surroundings. It's the most upscale Indian restaurant in town. White walls and big windows create an open, airy space. Bright upholstered banquette seats ring the walls and make a colorful accent. Artifacts and textiles from India provide sparse decoration.

If you love Mexican food, you ought to try Indian cuisine. Indian cooks rely less on tomato-based sauces, although you can find it in some dishes. You'll notice different spices, but few dishes are fiery hot. The spices are those of Asia: cilantro, cardamom, cinnamon, curry, and some pepper. Nuts and fruits may appear in some dishes, and there's lots of rice and occasional lentils. Your server will explain everything carefully so you can make the right choice. A good start for the novice is tandoori chicken. It's marinated and then baked in a tandoor oven. The marinade gives the chicken a deep red-orange color, but it's only color; tandoori chicken is not a spicy-hot dish. It's really a grilled chicken. If you prefer, try the tandoori shrimp for a change of pace.

Another trademark of Indian cuisine is delicious bread. The several varieties are unleavened, meaning flat, and served warm from the oven. Crisp lentil-flavored chips are delicious accompaniments. We like the curries and rice dishes known as biriyanis. Sag meat is delicious chunks of lamb stewed with spinach, another favorite. While you're waiting, walk over to the window at the kitchen to peer at the tandoor in operation. Or grab a seat at a sidewalk table and watch the Haymarket pedestrians.

The portions are generous; the beverage selection very good. Try the beers from India. We always find the lilting music and gentle atmosphere of this restaurant exactly to our tastes. Transport yourself to the exotic subcontinent—try the Oven.

Papa John's   *114 So. 14th*
Lincoln   *402-477-7657*

Papa John's has the familiar, bright, fluorescent look of a fast-food restaurant. Ordering at the counter adds to the fast-food atmosphere. But this isn't fast food; this is a Greek restaurant. Scattered among the brass trimmings are Greek posters. You can get American food, but that's like ordering hamburgers in Athens. There is a good salad bar with lots of Greek fixings. Go for the daily Greek specials. Our favorite is the Greek-style chicken; it's tender and juicy with a strong butter and lemon flavor. The Greek potatoes fried in olive oil and Greek spices are also uniquely tasty. The desserts, including golloutobourikio (vanilla custard cake), are terrific.

Piezano's

Lincoln

2740 South St.
402-474-3355

The *Lincoln Journal Star* calls Piezano's the best pizza joint in town. It's been hugely successful thanks to the mom-and-pop formula of Richard and Diane Berner. They devote countless hours each week to this modest restaurant with large carryout-delivery service. The recipes are authentic family Italian, and there's enough variety in the crusts and toppings to please everyone at your house. Don't overlook other menu items. They're awfully good, too.

PO Pears

Lincoln

322 So. 9th
402-476-8551

There are some places you have to see to believe. And in our opinion, at the top of the list is PO Pears. This is collectible heaven; the junk shop of eateries; the place where everything curious and wonderful winds up at one time or another. It's mainly a burger joint with unusual sandwiches served with fries. Nothing fancy. You have to get up and order yourself at the kitchen window. But, oh what a window! It's a wide-open mouth surrounded by a pair of enormous, red plastic lips. The kitchen will call your name when your order is up.

You could spend hours checking out this place. The Rube Goldberg bar could take several drinks to figure out, and the rooms stretch on and on. Lots of space to explore. Frankly, if it's been made, they've collected it. It's an after-work beer and conversation place and a college hangout, but they serve all ages. Get yourself down there. You can have an especially fine time when they host the adult spelling bee, a library fund-raiser. Hundreds of onlookers show up to watch friends knock themselves out for a good cause. PO Pears will show you just how much fun you could have had in school.

Rock 'N Roll Runza

14th & P Streets
402-474-2030

The Rock 'N Roll Runza is fun—fifties style. You're greeted by a teenager in fifties garb, probably on roller skates. The banter between staff members is straight out of another era. In fact, the kids can be downright disrespectful, but it's all in fun.

Rock 'N Roll Runza will transport you to the age of Elvis, hula hoops, and chocolate malts. Do Wop tunes boom over the sound system and fifties memorabilia decorate the establishment—Cary Grant movie posters, a Gene Autry/ Roy Rogers collage, neon signs, gas pumps, linoleum floors, and a soda fountain. A sign says Our Food Is So Good We Eat It Ourselves.

Each table has its own little jukebox. A quarter will override the tune on the loudspeaker. We stopped Little Eva's "Loco-Motion" dead in its tracks with The Big Bopper's classic "Chantilly Lace." After our selection, Little Richard bopped back over the speakers with "Long Tall Sally." We almost took off our shoes and danced—sock-hop style.

If you want to be cool, a soda fountain has the deadly drinks of the past—sodas and floats with names like Love Potion No. 9; phosphates called Suicides and Tutti-frutti; and a shake called The Big Red.

The food is a drive-in/country cafe hybrid. Our favorite is the meat loaf with real mashed potatoes and gravy, and bacon-seasoned green beans. There's also the breaded pork tenderloin, cheese frenchies, the best chili in town, and burgers you can customize with eleven extra toppings.

The Rock 'N Roll Runza is a hoot. It's fun for all ages. It'll have you snapping your fingers and singing songs from the past all the way home.

There are Runza restaurants all around Nebraska, but there's only one Rock 'N Roll Runza. The food at all Runza outlets is consistently good. If you're from another planet, you need to know that Runzas are a mixture of ground beef, cabbage, onions, and spices loaded in a loglike loaf of homemade-style dough. They're delicious! The burgers have been voted tops in Lincoln, and the chicken sandwiches and chili are right up there, too.

The Steak House
Lincoln

3441 Adams
402-466-2472

Fifty thousand steaks. That's about how many steaks the Steak House sells in one year. If you've eaten there, that's not hard to understand. The Steak House has all the ingredients of a great steakhouse. You know everything you need to know about the Steak House by breathing deeply. Begin when you step out of your car in the parking lot. By the time you step in the door, the aroma is overpowering, and you're properly prepared for big food—beefsteak.

The atmosphere is also a plus. There's the high ceiling, the rock walls covered with hunting trophies, a fireplace, an open grill, checkered tablecloths, and candles—it's a roadhouse/mountain lodge on Cornhusker Highway.

The steaks are superb, juicy, tender, and grilled to perfection. The Steak House has been around for 47 years. If they continue to sell 50,000 steaks a year for the next 40 years, that'll be another two million steaks. That's a lot of beef, and a lot of satisfied customers.

Taste of India
Lincoln

1320 O Street
402-475-1642

This O Street cafe doesn't receive the attention it deserves for good food at fair prices. Located in downtown Lincoln in the heart of the college-bar environs, it is easy to overlook in the evening when crowds throng the sidewalks out front. It does do a brisk lunch business with delicious specials that are served quickly. There's always one vegetarian special which we enjoy for a change of pace. This is a plain, modern, street-level dining room with big glass windows looking out on the sidewalk. Don't come here for the atmosphere; enjoy the food and fair prices. Then you can enjoy Indian food more often.

Ted and Wally's
Lincoln

701 P
402-477-7473

See Omaha listing.

Valentino's
Lincoln and elsewhere

see local listings

Valentino's used to dominate the Lincoln pizza scene. Since pizza competition has moved in, Val's continues to thrive largely because of its daily, all-you-can-eat Italian buffet. An Italian cornucopia, it's a monument to the favorite deadly sin—gluttony. It's where the Husker linemen would choose to eat on Sunday night.

The buffet table is about fifty feet long, and crammed with every imaginable Italian-American delicacy. You warm up with all kinds of salads, including lettuce and spinach, cold pasta salad, and fresh vegetables. Then you move on to chili, soup, pizza, spaghetti, cavatini, lasagna, tacos, etc., etc., etc.

166

You'll find the desserts, however, someplace else. Management has set them up on a separate trough, er, table.

We'll never forget one night at Val's. There were six Huskers crammed into a corner. For thirty minutes not a sound came from the table save the clank of cutlery, the grinding of six sets of molars, and the relentless movement of huge bodies back and forth from table to buffet, from buffet to table. Finally, at the end of the first half, one of the linemen, an All-American tackle, leaned back in satisfaction. Minutes passed, soon others joined him in a satisfied stupor. At long last full, they finally began talking.

There's not much else we need to say about Valentino's. A Nebraska-born franchise, it's everywhere. For consistent Italian-American fare; friendly, efficient service; attractive decor; and a relaxing, family-oriented atmosphere, Valentino's is hard to beat—even if you can't eat as much as a Husker lineman.

Vincenzo's Ristorante
Lincoln

808 P
402-435-3889

We like to gather with friends at Vincenzo's on a Friday night after work. It feels like we've come to the home of relatives on the Italian side of the family tree. They welcome us and feed our crowd like we're long-lost cousins. Right away the waiter brings us a ceramic pitcher of wine to help ourselves, family-style. Then later they have an honor system to pay by the glass. The pastas are plentiful with many choices of sauce and pasta. They also have other Italian entrees. No one goes away hungry, and you feel good about the simplicity of your food and the promptness with which it's served. Located in the Haymarket, the restaurant is an attractive destination. Sit up front in the bar area, if possible, so you can watch the parade of Haymarket visitors.

YiaYia's
Lincoln

1423 O St.
402-477-9166

At YiaYia's the feature is custom-made pizza—your choice of toppings, your choice of sauce. Sound like Pizza Hut? Not exactly. Want to challenge your taste buds? How about a combination of shrimp, garlic, jalapeno, almonds, cream cheese, turkey, walnuts, bell peppers, sun-dried tomatoes, and mozzarella cheese, all spread on a slather of green pesto sauce? Too much? Then order pepperoni and cheese. The menu lists over thirty different kinds of toppings (eight cheese choices), and four different light, sweet sauces (white, red, green pesto, and marinara). House specialties include the "Northern" with white sauce, mozzarella, Monterey Jack, Parmesan and Provolone, or the "Local" with hamburger, black olives, bacon, pepperoni, sausage, mushrooms, onions, bell peppers, and mozzarella.

The pizza at YiaYia's (grandmother in Greek, pronounced "ya-ya") is East Coast style, according to the owners. That means thin and crispy, prepared by hand with a wide assortment of unusual toppings. Whatever your choice, the pizza is different and tasty.

YiaYia's is located in a long, narrow building on O Street, Lincoln's main drag and the heart of the college bar scene. A thoughtful renovation kept the charm of the old building: rough brick walls, and high, tinned ceilings. Oak floors, an impressive front bar with a polished granite top, and indirect lighting combine to create a distinctive bar-bistro look. It is reminiscent of Italian neighborhood pizza parlors in Providence or New Haven. For distinctive but good pizza in an atmosphere a world apart from Pizza Hut, try YiaYia's.

Lunch at Jams Grill,
Omaha, Nebraska

—for Rick Barba, Richard Dooling, Richard Duggin,
and Brent Spencer, the "we" of the poem.

"We have come here Friday on a whim,"
I say. "Say, waited on by Angela."
Say she explains the specials on the run
from serving Coronas with lime, tequila.

By the time I've written these few lines
on my napkin with a borrowed pen
she's brought my special in record time
and gone to serve the lawyer at the end

of the bar. I never liked him anyway.
"This aint no *bare and ruined choir where late
the sweet birds sang*," we hear him say.
"We're all lawyers too," I lie. "We hate

guys like you." Angela says "Eat your food,
or I'll have to tell the cook it's just no good."

—Art Homer

Omaha

The old Market - Omaha

Robert Hanna

The Aquarium
Omaha

1850 S. 72nd St.
402-392-0777

The Aquarium is unique for fish, both to eat and to view. There's fine seafood on the menu and exotic, tropical fish in tanks displayed around the restaurant. It's a dark, cozy place. Watching the lolling fish slows life's pace and makes meals at the Aquarium a sensuous experience. You can order anything from trout to shark, from shrimp to snails, including lobster, oysters, and alligator. It's our pick for seafood in Omaha.

Cafe de Paris
Omaha

1228 So. 6th
402-344-0227

It costs at least $600 to fly to Paris for dinner. If you want to save your money, the closest thing to dinner in a small Parisian cafe is a trip to Omaha's Cafe de Paris.

The Cafe de Paris is Nebraska's entry into the culinary stratosphere. Elegant, gracious, attentive service could smother you. The food is, of course, French and laden with the basics of classic French cuisine—butter, cream, and fine wine.

Located in an unlikely looking small house, the cafe is tucked away in a semi-residential area on the south side of downtown. The unremarkable exterior offers no clue to the treasures inside. This restaurant recreates an era when dining was an art. Waiters hover, the linens are immaculate, and patrons feel as though they've just joined a very exclusive and very elegant private club. This is the time to use your best table manners and dress to the teeth. Although service quality is always high, you'll feel more comfortable if you look like you were born with a silver spoon in your mouth.

We recently celebrated special events—a marriage and a birthday—with friends at Cafe de Paris. The food, wine, and service were equal to the occasion. Our celebration, however, was a formal one. Go elsewhere for a casual, raucous night on the town.

This is Nebraska's top spot for the grand splurge, the perfect place to celebrate a really special occasion. But stand warned—it's expensive. Go only after winning the lottery. Also, it's no place for a diet meal. Entrees with all that butter and cream are stratospheric in terms of their calorie count, and the decadent desserts are definitely over the top. Not to worry. Just look at your bill and figure the calories-per-dollar ratio. You'll definitely get your money's worth.

Claudia's   *12129 W. Center Rd.*
Omaha   *402-330-3320*

We've always liked Claudia's. A food writer friend from Miami thought it was one of the best in the Midwest. Although owner Jack Churchill passed away recently, his legacy lives on with excellent continental cuisine. The emphasis is on French and Italian. The Caesar salad is still excellent.

Empanada House   *4109 L St.*
Omaha   *402-731-7368*

When we think of comfort, we think of the Empanada House. The only Chilean restaurant in the Midwest, it's a modest, friendly place that pampers the diner and makes you think seriously about packing for Chile the first chance you get. Owners Fulvia and Joaquin Leiva may be the best recruiters for Chile in the Northern Hemisphere. Joaquin, in particular, is the best salesperson around. You will not be able to tell him no.

The scale is intimate—low ceilings, tiny tables, seating for twenty, tops. Certainly not fancy. The effect is that of a storefront cafe in any small town in Chile. There's a little parking in back by the alley. Framed letters from local dignitaries and politicians are displayed proudly along with Chilean travel posters.

Joaquin is a most charming host. His life's mission is hospitality. He coddles his guests, patiently answers questions, and touts the cooking skills of his beloved wife, Fulvia. The flavorful commentary is nonstop. "Try our special milk drinks, perhaps leche con platanos? Milk mixed with fresh bananas; very good. We have our own sangria, good and refreshing. My favorite drink is vaina—wine blended with egg whites, vermouth and cinnamon. It's mixed up like a milk shake; very good, too." Joaquin makes each sound delicious, and unfortunately for the waistline, you'll want to try everything he suggests.

"What can Fulvia fix for you for dinner? Would you like our specialty—pastel de choclo, a meat and sweet corn dish baked in a clay server?" The pastel de choclo is one of our favorites. It's a novel experience combining shredded beef, chicken, spices, onions, a layer of grated sweet corn and milk that's then baked like a casserole.

On our first visit, a woman at the next table said, "This pastel is the best in the whole world." Her companion disagreed, claiming the restaurant's namesake, an empananda made of chicken, was superior. We nodded affirmation with mouths full, having sampled both.

The food is prepared fresh each day. The entrees are mild compared to some Mexican food. If you want some spice, however, a salsa can be ordered on the side. It'll provide some heat, but not enough to debilitate you or overwhelm Fulvia's delicate creations.

For dessert try the kuchen, a cake with a cooked fruit topping, a creation of early German immigrants to Chile. The sopaipillas Chilenas, somewhat like Mexican sopapillas, are flat, baked goods soaked in syrup and orange juice, then sprinkled with brown sugar.

When it's time to depart, the Leivas, dear friends from the time you walked in, will make you feel sorry to leave.

Flatiron   *1722 Howard*
Omaha   *402-344-3040*

The Flatiron is new, creative, and from the size of the crowds, successful. Built in 1911 by local banker Augustus F. Kountze, the Flatiron Building in downtown Omaha is an architectural treasure. This triangle-shaped building in the Georgian Revival style is listed in the National Register of Historic Places. The main floor where the restaurant is located has large glass windows providing street views from two of the three sides. The interior is modern with blacks and golds in contrast to the immaculate white tablecloths.

The food is even better than the decor. The menu is varied and sophisticated. We had a wonderful corn chowder with smoked chicken. Then we enjoyed a delicious steak in an exquisite wine sauce. The artistic presentation made the food too good to eat—at least for a few seconds.

176

The French Cafe

Early on, The French Cafe set the benchmark for sophistication and elegant dining in Nebraska. Twenty-five years ago it was a pioneer in its neighborhood, one of a handful of businesses in the Old Market of Omaha. The French Cafe brought continental cuisine and cafe society to palates accustomed to steakhouse fare. While dining at the French Cafe, you could believe, if just for a short while, that Nebraska was as sophisticated as any place on earth. Nebraskans discovered onion soup with tangy gruyere cheese and Caesar salads tossed at tableside, and a dark, spare atmosphere that felt, well, foreign, but wonderful.

In the past two decades, the food scene in Omaha has exploded with ethnic eateries, bistros, brew pubs, and a cornucopia of delightful dining, but if you want to visit le père et la mère of it all, you ought to go back to The French Cafe, where it all began.

So much remains the same. It's still dark and spare with brown walls and suspended lamps creating dim circles of light above each table. There are the oversized black and white photographs, although many more than before. You'll find the gargantuan bouquet of flowers and our favorite room just off the bar, where we like to enjoy cocktails and imagine ourselves in the drawing room of a magnificent château overlooking the Loire River valley.

The menu has gone through changes, naturally, but many of the old favorites remain—onion soup, crusty bread, an extensive wine list, and a variety of offerings worthy of a French bistro. The lunch menu is more casual than the evening fare, and even the dinner menu is simpler and more informal than it was two decades ago. This classic eatery deserves another visit. Come back to the Old Market and see how this fine French cafe has evolved. For as the French would say, "Plus ça change, plus c'est la même chose." The more things change, the more they are the same.

The Garden Cafe
Omaha, Lincoln, and elsewhere

see local listings

Ever wonder what the food's like in heaven? Here's our guess. It'll be delicious, fresh, and plentiful, prepared from scratch. There'll be variety at down-to-earth prices. It'll be served in a large, magical space that transports you to a garden filled with sparkling whites and soothing greens. There'll be friendly, smiling people of all types and ages. Wafting through the celestial atmosphere will be a mix of wonderful smells: cinnamon, almond, caramel, maple syrup, apples, fresh dough, butter, scrambled eggs, potatoes, ham, bacon, and sausage. Can you imagine it? Well, just think about a Garden Cafe. That's the best way we can describe it.

Back in 1985, the Garden Cafe opened in Rockbrook Village in Omaha. It started with a basic coffee-shop menu and added a few items each week. Word spread about gooey cinnamon rolls, cheesy potato casseroles, fresh raspberry pies, imaginative egg dishes, caramel bread pudding, and chicken-fried steak. Founder Ron Popp kept the phone lines humming as he tracked down family recipes to serve in his new restaurant. The Garden Cafe recreated the old-fashioned meals his Aunt Alice had prepared in Manilla, Iowa, and his mom had fixed in his hometown of Dow City. Soon sister Marvel's lemon bars, and Aunt Ethel's lemon meringue pie were customer favorites. Patrons came and returned, time and time again, eager to enjoy authentic midwestern food.

The Garden Cafe chain, a homegrown success story, continues to grow. At last count there were twelve Garden Cafes in four states.

Despite some recent corporate shuffles, the food and service remain unchanged. The Garden Cafe bustles, day or night, and its centerpiece is good food, attractively served in enormous quantities.

Our favorites include tasty waffles, smothered, as you can imagine, with heavenly clouds of whipped cream; any of twelve kinds of potato casseroles, but especially the Acapulco (spicy ground beef, chili, Mexi cheese sauce, tomatoes, onions, black olives, and sour cream with homemade salsa on the side). Even the orange juice is special—freshly squeezed, pulpy, and delicious. During our last visit, we had raisin french toast, thick slices dotted with raisins, crisp and golden brown, served with a warm pitcher of maple syrup. Our favorite dessert, of course, is the angel food cake.

Filled with coffee groups, business people in serious discussions, young families with children, teenagers, the Garden Cafes are the urban answer to the small-town eatery, and an old-fashioned bit of heaven. And just in case we don't make it to the pearly gates, we're going to enjoy this paradise on earth as often as possible.

La Strada 72
Omaha

3125 So. 72nd
402-397-8389

We always think about La Strada 72 as a restaurant for lovers. This is the place where we decided to marry. The atmosphere is classy, yet warm and comfortable. The main dining room is done in light colors with brick and blond wood, skylights, greenery, and the occasional mirror to create a light environment. Wonderful contemporary paintings are a special highlight. The patio off the dining room could become a favorite haunt. Tall brick walls, attractive landscaping, red chairs and faux-marble tables with bright-colored umbrellas create an inviting setting.

Always predictable, the food and service are not to be missed. Owners Subby and Nellie Floridia emigrated from Sicily, a southern Italian region known for spicy tomato sauces and good seafood. In their restaurant, however, they chose to feature northern Italian fare, a very popular alternative.

This restaurant is more upmarket than the many Omaha neighborhood trattorias, and we think that's exactly right. Expect elegant surroundings, first-class service, and exquisite, varied cuisine from this family-run business. Nellie and son Enzo are responsible for the kitchen. Subby, a diminutive, distinguished man who is well known as an Omaha barber, may be host in the evenings, or expect to find daughter Connie Pera. Like most great eateries, having the owners on hand ensures fine dining and the best customer service.

This restaurant receives consistently high marks. It deserves special mention and a loyal following among lovers of fine dining and any other lovers who may want a memorable night on the town.

M's Pub
Omaha

422 So. 11th
402-342-3550

Our favorite Old Market destination continues to be M's Pub. It has everything we want in a restaurant—good food, interesting people, charm, and a menu that embraces both lighter fare and full meals. The atmosphere feels casual but sophisticated without being stuffy. It's a pub and bistro in the best sense—a place to linger over conversation and to run into old friends, day after day. M's has following, and deservedly so.

This is an energetic, continental cafe. After two decades, its decor still delights with exposed brick, mirrors, and high ceilings. The big square bar attracts people at all hours, and the conversations are lively. The dining tables are located toward the back, but it's all quite intimate and no matter where you sit, you can't miss the action.

Many people come here just for cocktails, but you shouldn't ignore the food. Serving both lunch and dinner, M's is often crowded with patrons. Sometimes you may have to wait for a table, but pass the time perusing the great menu. The specials are worth trying, but we're partial to soups and M's always pleases with great choices. After soup, crusty bread, and a salad, we're often satiated, but don't let that stop you. Go for their veal or seafood specials. If your appetite is light, you can't go wrong with their Greek sandwich made of ground turkey.

We hope you will, too, embrace the delightful M's Pub.

The Market Basket
Omaha

Countryside Village
87th & Pacific
402-397-1100

There are big, fancy, expensive restaurants and bistros in Omaha, but we want to let you in on what we call our secret place, a delightful cafe and gourmet deli. Tucked away in Countryside Village on Pacific Street, the Market Basket is charming and cozy, but most important, its food is out of this world. We could go on and on about breakfasts of croissants filled with cheese, eggs, and ham; Normandy French toast; the French country breakfast; the omelettes with sides of fried potatoes, hash, bagels, or muffins—but we won't. We could write forever about creative and beautifully presented lunches with a dozen salads (How about wild rice, chicken, and pecans?), soups of all kinds, cold sandwiches galore (cheddar and crab), deli pastrami, and a burger served with homemade potato chips—but we won't. And for dinner, just trust us and let your imagination drift from pasta with fresh mushrooms, sun-dried tomatoes, artichokes, and a creamy tomato sauce to broiled salmon or chicken. And we haven't told you about dessert yet. No need.

Before we close, let us tell you about the best breakfast rolls on the planet. They're delectable, so good they're often gone by the time we roll into Omaha. They're a lighter version of sticky buns with a delicate maple flavor, and they epitomize the quality offered at the Market Basket. It's country gourmet food made from scratch and beyond compare. And if we lived in Omaha, we'd be the Market Basket's best customers.

Maxine's
Omaha

1616 Dodge
402-346-7600

Maxine's is perched atop one of Omaha's tallest buildings. With huge windows all around, this is one of the best dining views in the state. The dining room is plush; the food is excellent; and the flambe desserts are an attraction. The Sunday brunch is elegant.

Mister C's
Omaha

5319 No. 30th
402-451-1998

Someone said murals in restaurants are about as good as food in museums. You be the judge at Mister C's. There's an iridescent mural of Venice on one wall, and a backlit 3-D diorama of a Sicilian village on another. It's not great art, but it does set the bright theme of Mister C's. This theme is made even brighter by thousands of Christmas lights that shine year around. And there are even strolling musicians. The only thing missing in the Italian extravaganza is Pavarroti.

It's a huge place, but it always seems packed. It is so gaudy and whimsical that it makes you smile through your meal. That makes the food taste better and aids the digestion. The owner adds, "People feel so good here they just enjoy their meal." Other things that make them feel good about Mister C's are the wide selection of typical Italian specialties (including a memorable minestrone soup), large servings, and reasonable prices.

The real Mr. C adds to the year-round holiday atmosphere by greeting guests personally. He's a jolly man, and dressed in the proper attire, he could pass for Santa.

Nettie's
Bellevue

7110 Railroad Ave.
402-733-3359

One of our tests for a good Mexican place is the tamales. Many so-called authentic Mexican places don't even serve tamales. Nettie's does. And get this, Huskers, they're even served in cornhusks. The fare at Nettie's continues in a quality vein from there. The chile and guacamole are excellent, the beef and pork are fresh, and the dishes have a spicy, alive flavor—before the salsa—that we like in our Mexican food. The servings are large, but the prices are relatively modest.

Old Vienna Cafe
Omaha

4829 So. 24th
402-733-7491

4829 So. 24th
402-733-7491

To find an authentic South Omaha hangout, go to the Old Vienna Cafe. The atmosphere is dark with mahogany paneling, Austrian scenes on the walls, and European banners and posters suspended from the ceiling. A collection of wine and beer bottles is crammed into every remaining space. Except for a few tables for bar service near the front door, the dinner tables are set formally with white linen tablecloths, red napkins, and unmatched china. Classical music adds a perfect touch.

The wine list is extensive, with the traditional European emphasis on age and quality. Walter seems to get a lot of pleasure out of presenting his suggestions for wine with each entree, and he has a wide selection to offer. He can offer reasonably-priced house wines by the glass or an extravagant bottle for mega-bucks.

The food at the Cafe doesn't disappoint. The emphasis is on Austrian and German dishes, particularly veal. Eight different veal dishes are served. The menu has three selections of weinershnitzel and such dishes as Vienna goulash. The entrees are embellished with exquisite sauces.

Whether you're a wine connoisseur, gourmet, or a seeker of offbeat cafes, you'll enjoy South Omaha's version of old Vienna.

Spanna
Omaha

132nd & West Dodge Road
402-493-7606

Spanna sets the standard for excellence in cooking and presentation. This suburban location attracts crowds both at lunch and dinner, and it's easy to see why. The menu is inventive and varied with the season. The specials are always first-rate, but the regular menu fare will also please. On occasion, we will split a pasta as a first course to leave room for the surprises to come. The surprise is always a delicious, fresh taste and exquisite presentation.

The decor here is casual and colorful. The prices are beyond those of a small-town cafe, but certainly not outrageous when compared with big city dining outside the state. We think all real foodies in Nebraska should stake out Spanna's. It doesn't get much better than this.

Stella's   *106 Galvin Rd. South*
Bellevue   *402-291-6088*

At Burger King you have it your way. At Stella's you get it their way. The menu is limited—burgers, grilled cheese, fries, maybe a special. That's it. And don't be asking for lettuce, tomato, and special sauce. If you want P & O—pickles and onions—there's a small fee. Put your condiments on yourself. And don't be askin' for no tablecloths, placemats, plates, knives, forks, and fancy napkins. There are napkins, but they're the plates. Everything, except the fries, is served on a napkin.

It's a low-overhead place. No unneeded decorating expense here; the dominant orange theme seems as if it's been there forever. But low overhead means low price. The last time we were there nothing cost more than two bucks. The gigantic and tasty burgers are powered by a taste we'll call juicy rather than greasy. They're big uns; they lop out of the bun. The fries are tasty, too.

Stella's is honest as a bar and grill can be. If you don't like the chow, and the building could talk, it simply would say, "Frankly my dear, I don't give a damn."

Ted and Wally's

see local listings

Omaha's Old Market
Lincoln's Haymarket

For ice cream, real homemade ice cream, you can't beat Ted and Wally's. Ted and Wally's high-ceilinged store nestled among a cluster of historic buildings in the Old Market, is spacious and bright. The interior is as happy as the looks on the customers' faces when they take their first creamy bite. The ice cream is made right before your eyes with churns packed with rock salt and ice. They make about 200 gallons a week. You can get everything from cinnamon to banana bubble gum. The most unique variety is French toast. It's a delicious mixture of ice cream, bread, egg custard, and maple syrup. Ted and Wally's is a nostalgic trip back to an old-fashioned ice cream store. There is also a store located in the Haymarket area of Lincoln.

V. Mertz

1022 Howard Street
402-345-8980

Omaha

V. Mertz is another Omaha institution where food and exquisite service make a difference. For two decades, V. Mertz has been known as one of Omaha's finest restaurants for its consistent quality.

It also may be one of the most romantic. Nestled in the Old Market Passageway, it's dark, remote, and inviting. It reminds us of dining somewhere in a European wine cellar, which is appropriate because it offers the best wine list in Omaha. Located in a 100-year-old building, originally a warehouse, the restaurant has abundant charm in a magical setting.

People who love fine dining and who know a lot about cooking should relish this bistro for its varied offerings and attention to detail. It's signature dish is the V. Mertz peppersteak, but there are daily menu changes worth exploring. Seafood, lamb, pork, veal, fowl, and beef are among the offerings. Not to be missed are great side dishes that are both inventive and delicious.

This can be a pricey destination. The lunch menu is more reasonable, but who'd want to go back to work after such a splendid interlude?

Vivace   *1110 Howard Street*
Omaha   *402-342-2050*

Vivace's is a newer destination in Omaha's Old Market. The owners of the magnificent M's Pub also operate this establishment. We like its casual, upscale atmosphere and interesting take on the pasta theme. The menu is quite varied. For example, you can order any of twenty-four sauces with a handful of specialty pastas. But this is not a traditional all-you-can-eat spaghetti house. The fare is contemporary with many unusual ingredients. In addition to pizza and pasta, Mediterranean fare is a specialty. Try the tapas, little morsels favored by diners in Spain, and the meal of choice for grazers. Another Spanish national dish is paella, saffron rice, and seafood cooked together in a large pan. Risotto and couscous are also featured. There is something for everyone on this menu.

We like the decor with its exposed brick walls, wooden floors, and eclectic art. The best tables are up front where you can watch the passing crowds stroll by.

Zio's
Omaha

7924 W. Dodge / 402-391-1881
12463 W. Center / 402-330-1444

Zio's was voted best pizza in town by the *Omaha World-Herald's* "Toast of the Town" survey. Omahans seem to like their pizza New York-style—hand tossed, and thin, and crispy in the center with a thick edge. They also like being able to craft their own pie from about 30 different toppings. There are the standards: pepperoni, hamburger, and anchovy. Or there are pesto toppings with chicken and shrimp. For the vegetarians the Garden Special has eggplant, zucchini, mushrooms, green peppers, red onions, extra cheese, and broccoli. If you want something other than pizza, try calzone. These are turnovers stuffed with cheese and toppings, and drenched on the outside with sauce, cheese, and more toppings.

Barbecue Omaha

Barbecue aficionados are addicted. Maybe it's the smoke. But whatever it is, barbecue brings out strange behavior in otherwise reasonably normal people. We have a friend so frugal he will walk ten blocks to the grocery store. Yet he's been known to drive one hundred miles to check out a rumor that a new barbecue joint serves ribs with a smoky pull so strong that "Q" purists refuse to disguise their flavor with sauce. If you have even a hint of this problem, jump in the car and check out this triad of Omaha barbecue favorites:

Jim's Rib Haven
3801 Ames Avenue
402-451-8061

Featured in the travel section of the *New York Times,* Jim's is Omaha's best-kept barbecue secret, many claim.

Old Mill Barbecue
10870 West Dodge Rd.
402-496-7427

Slow-cooked, hickory-smoked barbecue in vast quantities. You can choose from three tomato-based sauces, or an unusual yellow vinegar sauce. The baked beans and cole-slaw are good sides. The place is awfully hygienic for a barbecue place, but somehow it doesn't seem to detract from the taste.

Skeet's
2201 N. 24th Street
402-344-3420

The veteran of Omaha barbecue, Skeet's has served good Southern barbecue for over 40 years.

Ethnic Eateries

Ethnic eateries abound in Omaha. Here are some of our favorites.

Afghani-Kabob

3023 Farnam
402-346-4410

The only authentic Afghan restaurant in Omaha, the Afghani-Kabob, will whisk you away to the desert. You'll even feel like a hungry nomad when you sit shoeless on pillows at low tables under the "party tent" at the back. Like Ahmad's, the food is prepared with herbs and spices, with no grease and little fat. Kabobs are the specialty, with "c" spices dominating: cayenne, curry, cilantro, cardamom, and cumin. The food can be very hot, particularly the garlic pepper yogurt sauce. If you like condiments, order the chutney. It is not as thick and sweet as the Indian variety, but very tasty. The entrees are very reasonably priced and come with rice, soup or salad, and a vegetable.

Ahmad's

1006 Howard
402-341-9616

Owner Ahmad Nazaraghaie sets the friendly tone when you visit his tiny Persian restaurant in the Old Market. As our daughter Karen put it, "He treats you like a guest in his home." The atmosphere at Ahmad's is also inviting—wood floors, high ceilings, and soothing blue walls, blue table-cloths, Persian rugs, trays, and Persian-style paintings. Persian string music completes the Middle Eastern mood.

For the health conscious, Ahmad's is perfect. Ahmad does much of the cooking, which is low in fat. The meats are steamed, not fried, or even cooked with oil. Although healthy, the dishes are beautifully flavored by a variety of delicate Eastern spices. The appetizers, like hummus and falafel, get you off to an exuberant start. The entrees range from tender, boneless chicken in a sweet and sour walnut-pomegranate sauce to kabobs of all kinds.

Ahmad's is a great place to relax; the food is tasty, and Ahmad will make your stay an enjoyable one. The pace is slow, so just sit back and watch the people stroll by in the Old Market.

Bohemian Cafe
1406 So. 13th
402-342-9838

In operation since 1924, the Bohemian Cafe is one of Nebraska's most enduring ethnic restaurants. Starting with "Vitame Vas" (we welcome you) at the front door and continuing with carvings, flowers and glassware, the decor creates a Bohemian atmosphere, enhanced by servers wearing brightly colored dresses. You can get the usual Czech specialties, sauerbraten, roast duck, sauerkraut, plum dumplings, rabbit, and a lot more. This is hearty, belly-busting fare at prices that are downright reasonable. Czech it out.

Butsy LeDoux's
1014 Howard
402-346-5100

Lacking in culinary courage? Then perhaps Butsy LeDoux's is not for you. This is a place for the adventurous. Here's a place that promises to take your taste buds on a roller-coaster ride. There are spicy gumbos, jambalaya, the muffletta sandwich, and one of our favorites—voodoo stew— a bewitching blend of beef, okra, tomatoes, onions, spinach, red beans, and special seasonings. If you're really adventurous, on occasion you can get boiled crayfish. We've found that it's one of those try-it-once, that's-enough specialities of the deep South. You can also order blackened dishes, if you care to do that to your food. Much of our cooking at home turns out that way so we don't order it when we go out. Eating at Butsy's is the next best thing to eating in Lafayette, Louisiana. As they say down there, we "guar-onn-tee it."

Chez Chong

1015 S. 10th
402-346-3635

Not a Chinese restaurant, Chez Chong considers itself Southeast Asian, featuring the dishes of Thailand, Malaysia, Singapore, and Vietnam, but with a strong French influence. The food is spicy with lots of lime, lemon grass, and other Asian seasonings. Examples of the dishes representing a wide variety of countries are Vietnamese spring rolls, Thai soup (hot and spicy), and the French coquilles St. Jacques or rabbit. This is beautifully prepared Asian gourmet at substantial prices.

El Alamo

4917 So. 24th
402-731-8969

This is the best and most authentic Mexican restaurant in Omaha. When you go to a place frequented by a predominance of Hispanic families, you know you're in the right place. None of that Tex-Mex microwave fare, this is the real enchilada. A wide variety of choices, and at bargain prices.

Food Gallery

312 S. 72nd
402-393-4168

Although often referred to as an Arabian restaurant, the Food Gallery features an eclectic mixture of Lebanese,

French, and Syrian recipes, owner Albert Saigh informed us. Whatever the mix, it's tasty. Many of the menu items are vegetarian, however, there are also several chicken and lamb dishes. We reveled in baba ghanouj, a chick-pea dip with tastes of garlic, butter, and lemon. It's served with a flat bread for dipping. *Omaha World-Herald* food writer Jim Delmont really knows fine cuisine, so when he raved about the Food Gallery's seafood bisque soup, we jumped in the car and headed to Omaha. Here's how Jim described this fantastic soup: "This is a rich, delectable seafood bisque ($4.95). It takes Saigh hours to prepare a lobster stock that eventually is blended with a cream sauce, sherry, lobster, and shrimp. The result is a soup worthy of the finest restaurants in Chicago or New Orleans. It's memorable!" The soup was well worth the drive from Lincoln.

Greek Islands
3821 Center St.
402-346-1528

We've never been to the Greek Islands when it wasn't crowded. Why? It's a casual, inviting, neighborhood restaurant. Someone from the Sgourakis family is always there to make sure everything is just right. The food comes in a wide variety of selections and the servings are huge. Finally, the prices for this tasty Greek fare are very modest. From feta to moussaka to the final bite of baklava, you will enjoy a trip to the Greek islands, or rather the Greek Islands in Omaha.

H and I Cafe
1905 Farnam
402-345-8877

Thai food has more flavors per bite than any other cuisine in the world. And the H and I Cafe is one of the best Thai restaurants we've tried. When you taste one of the dishes you might find the flavors of cilantro, lime, onion, peppers, peanut, and lemon grass all wrapped into one scintillating flavor burst. This simple cafe, successful in its small quarters on South 24th Street, has moved uptown. Of course, they have pad thai and the other Thai standards, but their curries are also outstanding. The panang nna gai includes chicken with sautéed sweet curry and coconut milk. It is spicy, hot, and delicious. If you haven't eaten at the H and I, you're missing something.

Imperial Palace

11200 Davenport
402-330-3888

The decor at the Imperial Palace is elaborate and massive. You feel like you're in a Chinese palace. The menu is huge, the service outstanding, and the Chinese food is as good as any in Omaha. The pork dishes stand out, as well as the Peking duck and Beggar's chicken, a whole chicken stuffed with vegetables and cooked after being covered with clay. There are also exotic off-menu dishes to try if you want to get daring.

Indian Oven

1010 Howard
402-342-4856

The atmosphere at the Indian Oven, including the smell of exotic spices, transports you to India. Lovers of unusual fare will find Indian cuisine much to their liking. Rice is a staple accompanied by stewed meat dishes much the way it is served in Chinese restaurants. The delicacy of the spices and flavorful aromas are unlike any other exotic food. Lamb is always a good choice, curried or not. Enjoy interesting mixtures of stewed vegetables and delicious breads. Because Indian food seems exotic and unfamiliar, it doesn't mean that it should be saved for rare occasions. It's hearty and healthy, and a good place to enjoy it is the Indian Oven. Try to get a seat in the upstairs garden room, a little Indian solarium. Specialties: Curries, tandoories, and breads.

Jaipur
10922 Elm St.
402-392-7331

Jaipur is tastefully decorated with a warm, dark atmosphere emphasizing soothing green colors and tasteful Indian art and artifacts on the walls. A dominating mural of a tiger hunt covers the east wall. Chef Raj Bhandari is Nebraska's best Indian chef. His food can be delicate, hot, and spicy, and the variety of the menu is enormous. Try the jalapeno-flavored home brew. This is one of Omaha's finest.

Neighborhood Italian

Omaha is loaded with great neighborhood Italian restaurants. Here's a quick rundown of some of our favorites. They're all good, so try them and see what you think.

Frankie and Phyl's

1208 S. 24th
402-342-9721

This is a friendly, workingman's Italian cafe on South 24th Street. The conversation at the next table went like this: "You get a good wage, you work hard. You don't get a good wage, you don't work so hard." A picture of Marlon Brando as the Godfather hangs behind the counter. Specialty: Polpetti for $5.25. It's like a hamburger steak, but with egg, bread crumbs, and Italian spices. A red sauce covers the top.

Leonarda's

3852 Leavenworth
402-346-5464

We like to go Leonarda's when it's cold. The inside is cozy with a high, tin ceiling, beams, red tablecloths, pleasant music, and a slow-paced, relaxed atmosphere. The cooking is warming and very authentic Sicilian. The sauces aren't just sauces; they're loaded with additional taste. The Alfredo has mushrooms; another sauce has tomatoes and basil; the meat sauce has peas and onions. Leonarda's is nothing fancy, but in the final analysis, it's consistency rather than panache that is the hallmark of a good restaurant. Specialties: Veal, chicken and scampi.

Lo Sole Mio

3001 S. 32nd Ave.
402-345-5656

This residential restaurant is thought by some to be the best Italian eatery in town. Special touches include a bottle of red wine on each table, with diners charged for what they drink. Warm olive oil is served for delicious bread dipping. The sauces—marinara, cream, carbonara, Alfredo, and primavera set Chef Losole's cooking apart. There is pasta galore, six different choices. It's truly an Italian family-operated bistro; there are more than a dozen members of the Losole family involved in the operation. Specialties: Pastas and lasagna.

Raphael's

1217 S. 13th
402-341-9010

Raphael's success is measured by the fact that it started as a tiny storefront, and now has expanded with an attractive dining room. When you look around, you'll see that almost everyone is eating pasta. But there are lots of other choices. Raphael's features southern Italian cooking. Its marinara sauce is a highlight. Specialties: Pastas, Sicilian chicken, muffletta sandwich.

Sons Of Italy Hall

1288 So. 10th Street

Oops! This isn't a small neighborhood restaurant. It isn't even a restaurant. But we had to include it just for its fun and uniqueness. It's open only on Thursday at noon, but it's great fun, especially right before an election when politicians storm the place. They are allowed to shake hands only outside the hall. Open for lunch only on the last Thursday of the month in the summer, the eatery relies on volunteers to serve the 600 to 700 people who come for pasta. Some of the volunteers wear shirts that say "Italian and Proud of It" or "Butch Sez: 'Quit throwin the forks away.'" One of the volunteers we talked to was Czech.

Jump in line. Although the food isn't gourmet and is served on paper plates, it costs only about five bucks. The dish of the day varies from week to week, but it's always some kind of pasta with salad, bread, and coffee. And there are freebies. As we walked out, a politician running for M.U.D. gave us a pocket calendar. Specialties: pasta and politicians.

Villa Fiorita
2413 S. 13th St.
402-346-0206

Villa Fiorita is an intimate one-room, mom-and-pop cafe featuring Sicilian cooking. Its essence is olive oil, herbs and spices, lemon, capers, and vinegar. The quantities are large and the prices are modest. The owners and concerned staff take a special interest in the meals: "Was everything to your liking?" the owner asks with a concerned look, and then relaxes visibly when you assure that everything was just fine. Specialties: Double-crust Sicilian pizza, sausage, pasta, Sicilian bread.

Omaha Steakhouses

Trying to pick the best steakhouse in the old stockyards town of Omaha is like trying to pick which beefy Husker offensive lineman is the best blocker. So what do you do? You put them all on your All-American team. Here are our brief selections:

Angie's
1001 Pacific
402-341-8800

Angie's was voted Omaha's best business lunch spot. Where else is the most expensive item on the luncheon menu a luncheon steak for around six bucks? The owner claims his sides of spaghetti are the best in Omaha.

Caniglias
1114 S. Seventh
402-341-7778

This is a smaller, extremely casual, neighborhood steakhouse still here after fifty years. The steaks are good, and sides of pasta or vegetables, potatoes, salad bar, toasted ravioli, homemade soup, and Italian bread will fill you up even without the steak. The steak prices are probably the lowest in town.

Gorat's
4917 Center
402-551-3733

A good friend, Dick Knudsen, grew up near Gorat's. He and his lovely wife, Sally, invited us to try it out one cold January night. We're glad we did. It's one of Omaha's best. Gorat's is large, the service is prompt and friendly, and the steaks, aged in their coolers, are terrific. As I recall we also had two rare appetizers, fried parsley and fried artichoke hearts.

Johnny's Cafe   *4702 So. 27th*
                                                           402-731-4774

Omaha's classiest, and oldest, continuous steakhouse.

Omaha Prime   *415 S. 11th*
                                                           402-341-7040

The Omaha Prime is but a babe compared to the venerable,
old steakhouses listed above, but it's a comer. The dark wood
interior with heavy beams provides an atmosphere of an old-
line steakhouse in New York or Denver that belies its youth.
The "strictly prime" steaks are expensive, but superb. The
menu items, even the side dishes, are a la carte. One trendy
feature is a glass-walled, cigar-smoking room.

Ross'   *909 S. 72nd*
                                                           402-393-2030

Huge but comfortable describes Ross', Omaha's steakhouse
supreme. Like most of the good ones, it's been around for
ages, forty years to be exact. The T-bone is their specialty
and the chateaubriand for two is also outstanding. The
steaks are large, and you can specify larger cuts if you wish.
We sometimes take steak for granted in Nebraska. But lest
we forget, Ross' is one of the best in the world's best steak
area.

The M and L Cafe

Her body no heavier than half a dozen sticks,
Mrs. Martin had outlived everybody,
her life shrunk to a bedroom on the first floor
of her half-empty house. She came afternoons
to a booth in my mother's cafe, my mother

finding that what Mrs. Martin really wanted
was coffee with cream and sugar and a soft
hamburger bun. Sugar in the bottom
of the cup, the sound of stirring

in the cafe in the afternoon, the sound
of my mother rolling pie dough.
Mrs. Martin chewing, toothless,
knot of her headscarf wobbling under her chin,
big knuckles, big brow bones. My mother
charged her fifteen cents, the dime and
the nickel beside the saucer, the coffee

and the afternoon half-finished, my mother
wiping flour from her hands, coming
out of the kitchen to talk.

—Marjorie Saiser

Condiments

Hotel Wilber · Wilber, Ne.

My Favorite Dives

Philosopher John Dryden must have been referring to out-of-the-way, hole-in-the-wall restaurants when he wrote, "He who would search for pearls must DIVE below." That's what makes looking for dives so much fun. They're jewels in the depths waiting to be discovered. To find them takes an adventurous spirit—and sometimes a strong stomach.

How do you know when you've wandered into a dive? First there's the walk-in test. Look around. Dives are usually dark. Breathe in, but not too deeply. Dives reek of smoke and the smell of grease redolent; you can almost feel your arteries slam shut.

Other techniques help discern a dive. Try these sit-down tests: If there's a bug in your beer instead of lemon in your water, it's a dive. If you hear "Will that do it?" instead of "Enjoy," it's a dive. If the bartender is as grumpy as a bucking bull with jock itch, it's a dive. If the waitress isn't slow, the floor's just sticky, it's a dive. If spaghetti is called finger food, it's a dive. And so it goes.

A dive is an evolutionary throwback to a time before fast food, nouvelle food, artistically-presented food, basil-this food and haute cuisine food. Dives don't offer pasta, it's plain spaghetti; they don't serve au gratin, it comes with cheese; they don't have au jus, they serve just grease. Although joints are allowed great leeway when it comes to menus, or a lack of them, sandwiches are pretty much a standard.

A dive is a place where your plate overflows with a very large portion of decent, bare-knuckled food, accompanied by good-hearted, although not always good-natured, service. Dives result in a full stomach that brings joy—and sometimes a burn—to the heart.

Now don't get us wrong. We love dives. There's something very honest about a dive. No pretenses, no frills, no false elegance; no hostesses, no tablecloths, and sometimes no menus. Just simple, plain, comfort—the same kind of comfort you find in your favorite pair of well-worn house slippers.

There are lots of great dives in Nebraska. The epitome of a great dive was Lebsack's, located on P Street in Lincoln. Their specialty was beef and cheese sandwiches, and greasy chili. (Barrymore's in Lincoln patterns its chili recipe after its key ingredient—grease.) Big Ed Lebsack, bald, with the voice of a professional hog caller, did the bartending. If you asked him for coffee, he'd say, "This is a beer joint; we don't serve coffee." Hank was in the back doing the cooking in a tiny kitchen area so clean you could have eaten off the floor. John, thin with an undertaker's sense of humor, was the sole waiter. One waiter was enough—the service he provided didn't take long.

There wasn't anything healthy about the food. Health aside, it did taste good, and the formula was successful. Lebsack's had a packed house for lunch, and you had to get there by 10 a.m. on football game days if you wanted to get in.

The chili was accompanied by a spartan ration of oyster crackers, stapled in a little glassine envelope—a pre-cellophane artifact. You had to be darned careful not to dump the staple in your chili. If you asked for anything John hadn't thrown on the table, you were likely to get a mumble that made it clear you'd better go elsewhere if you wanted special service. A friend used to bug John by asking for the pie of the day. John's sour reply: "You want that stuff. Go over to Miller and Paine."

Lebsack's is gone, but premier dives remain in Nebraska. Ted's Tea Room, a Columbus bar, deserves a visit based on the name alone. There's never been a teatime in that hole-in-the-wall.

A good dive in downtown Lincoln is The Watering Hole. Its buffalo wings, described as "awesome," smack of vinegar and hot sauce. It's a good place to soak up small-town atmosphere in the midst of the college bar scene.

The Endacott pick for favorite Nebraska dive is the Blue River Inn in Endicott. (No namesake here.) Its decor is superior to the understated motif of most dives. The inn is a junk shop turned eatery. Owned by Bob and Catherine Shelburne, it features such attractions as a two-headed calf, a cigar-store Indian, stuffed animals, and an extensive bottle collection. There are five old stoves. A sign reads "Wanted, free cobs for fire."

"It's a general store, dry goods, short order lunch, and gas place," reports Bob Shelburne, a droll but grizzled character in sleeveless T-shirt, baggy trousers, and a battered cowboy hat.

Coffee is available in the morning, but the only formal meal is lunch. At noon, onions and pickles are placed in Tupperware bowls on unmatched tables and chairs. The limited menu is written on a piece of paper and tacked on the wall. There are burgers, of course, fries, and usually a daily special. The customers are farmers, local businessmen, traveling salesmen, and the occasional L.A. developer. A friend who recommended this culinary outpost explains: "Hotshot developers from L.A. fly in to pick out bricks at Endicott Clay Products and then insist on going to the Inn for lunch. They think it's a funky place."

"They just eat what I fix," Catherine says. "No caviar or champagne," Bob booms.

A classic dive, it fascinates because of the many odd items packed into a little space. The owners and customers, refugees from an O. Henry story, create an ambience that's nothing if not informal. It's these extra attractions—plus the satisfaction of finding a pearl in the world of dives—that makes the food taste even better.

Driving Nebraska
Francis Moul

Get off the Interstate.

Anyone wanting to take a windshield tour of the strange and fascinating roads of Nebraska should get off I-80 right away. Interstate 80 is the direct descendant of the Platte River Road, which in covered wagon days ran along the so-called Nebraska Coast, following the Platte River Valley. This was an easily traveled road, flat and close to water and trees, and devoid of major hills and impediments. While that was great for ox-drawn carts, today's high speed travelers are bored easily by the unimaginative terrain. (Clyde Brion Davis, a journalist and author born at Unadilla, Nebraska, even wrote a novel called *Nebraska Coast*.)

To know the real delights of Nebraska geography journey along some of the roads described here. And remember, for every trail you explore, there are many more to discover—just look for the fainter black solid and dotted lines on the official state map. The map also gives clues to finding marvelous scenery, so pay close attention to the various colors that denote geological differences in the state.

The most famous and unique part of Nebraska is the Sandhills. These 24,000 square miles of grass-covered sand dunes hold a special place in Nebraska geography, even though they are populated by fewer than one person per square mile. There are many Sandhills roads to travel. U.S. Highway 2 has been designated one of the nation's top ten beautiful highways; it cuts diagonally across the Sandhills from Grand Island to Crawford. It is an easy drive that takes you from the dissected plains to the Sandhills themselves, with waterfowl-covered wetlands and cattle towns like Hyannis interspersed among the omnipresent hills of sand.

To really see the Sandhills as they should be seen, veer onto a typical one-lane road. It may be paved but more likely will be graded gravel or sand. Drive the latter only in dry weather—beware of wet or snowy roads. My favorite Sandhills road is north of North Platte on Nebraska Highway 97, then west on Nebraska Highway 92 about eighteen miles. It will be the first paved road west of Tryon, heading north. It crosses both forks of the Dismal River. The North Fork is the easiest to find and is worth a stop for the view and to listen to the birds. Also stop at the top of any long hill to get out and enjoy the isolated splendor. Pull over to the right at the top of each hill, in case of an approaching vehicle, though you may not see another traveler during the whole trip. The road gets back to Highway 97 just south of Mullen. The middle portion is not paved and looks like a ranch road. Keep going.

A short trip to see the splendors of the dissected loess hills also starts on Highway 92 at Arnold. The Arnold-Dunning road goes north out of Arnold and within a few miles you reach the highest point in Custer County at Devil's Creek. Stop near the guardrails, pulling well off the road, and get out to look. On the east is the broken-up Devil's Den (better described as the Devil's Playground) of beautiful cut-up hills and canyons. On the left is one of the best long distance views of both the dissected plains and the Sandhills, farther away. If you are lucky, you will see a red-tailed hawk circling over the canyon and dark storm clouds piled high above. You can then travel on to Dunning or return to Arnold.

South of Interstate 80 are the best examples of the dissected loess hills. These are made up of fine soils that were borne by water and wind from sources north and west of Nebraska anywhere from 20,000 to 8,000 years ago. The Sandhills are made up of heavier grains of sand that were deposited first. The loess soil carried a bit farther. The plains of loess soil, up to 200 feet thick, have since been carved-up by wind and water into what can be called the Nebraska Canyonlands. Take the road south of the Brady exit on I-80. It is paved for a while and goes past Jeffrey Lake, a reservoir that is worth exploring. Then continue south. A network of roads will take you past a prairie dog town, lots of wildlife, and some of the most beautiful Nebraska scenery outside of the Pine Ridge area. The less adventurous should travel U.S. Highway 83 between North Platte and McCook for examples of the same sights.

At Maywood on Highway 83, find the broken-line road to Hayes Center. That gives you the scenic flavor of both the Sandhills and dissected plains, and takes you to the famous campsite of Duke Alexis. In 1871 President U.S. Grant sent out word that Grand Duke Alexis of Russia wanted to hunt buffalo on his American tour. Gen. George Custer arranged a hunt, held during an unseasonably warm January in 1872, guided by Buffalo Bill with the help of Chief Spotted Tail and his band of Sioux Indians (who really found the buffalo to hunt). You can visit the actual site by following signs along the county road, about nine miles northeast of Hayes Center. The way in can be a treacherous drive, so be prepared for a walk.

In the beautiful Pine Ridge area of northwest Nebraska many roads are scenic and a map of federal lands from the U.S. Forest Service in Chadron is well worth the $4 price for its accurate details. The best of the best roads, however, is through Sow Belly Canyon. You'll find this just north of Harrison in Sioux County, the first turn east. Follow it through the canyon, with a stop at Coffee Park, and even a climb up the bluffs there, then head back south along Pants Butte Road for breathtaking views.

On the opposite side of the state, the Missouri River bluffs give the best views, and are most enjoyable in the fall when leaves turn colors. There are many roads to follow; from Nebraska City take the road south from Highway 2 just east of U.S. Highway 75. Wind around the county gravel roads to Peru and Brownville, but don't miss Indian Cave State Park for the best of the best scenery on this end of the state.

Niobrara State Park serves the same purpose in northeast Nebraska, with magnificent high views of the Missouri River valley. Explore roads in and out of Ponca State Park as well. You may be able to find an extinct volcano there, but you'll have to look hard.

The best advice to tour Nebraska and really, really see it: find the new, colored official state map and look for black, broken lines. On these roads you will find few vehicles, hardly any amenities or rest stops, and tiny towns with maybe a store or gas station. But, you will see pristine scenery that will fill your memory tank forever, any season of the year. But be careful of roads with Minimum Maintenance signs, muddy or snowy conditions, and traveling with an emptying gas tank. If you do get lost, keep exploring. You'll find pavement eventually, and you will have seen the very best of the best.

Francis Moul is a retired Nebraska publisher, a Ph.D. candidate in history at the University of Nebraska-Lincoln and a passioned driver of Nebraska roads.

Dining on the MoPac East Trail

Richard Conradt

Are you tired of sitting at home eating the same old hash? Are your friends urging you to try something new? If that's true, why not plan an adventure along the MoPac Trail, a hiker-biker trail running east of Lincoln along the abandoned Rock Island Railroad line. The towns of Walton, Eagle, and Elmwood are located on the trail and each boasts several eateries that offer a wide selection.

Many people are aware of the Walton Trail Company, a bike shop/trail stop, located in the small town of Walton, just three miles east of 84th Street. Fresh and interesting, the Walton Trail company is housed in a 100-year-old wooden building adorned with vintage bicycles and other cycling paraphernalia. It offers fresh air and down home eats. The menu includes the best (and only) sandwiches in Walton, cold refreshments, gourmet coffees and teas, as well as other items of sustenance. The Walton Trail Company is open till sundown seven days a week. Prices are reasonable and the fresh air is free.

Eagle, a very "eater friendly" environment, is the next town on the MoPac Trail, just eight short miles from Walton. This small town supports four successful dining establishments: Mister Henry's, Cafe Carrera, Golden Eagle Keno Lounge, and Grandma's House.

Mister Henry's, at Fourth and Main, is a restaurant and lounge offering a homey atmosphere for dining. I've had the pleasure of trying several menu items, most notably the soup and salad bar, an expanse of greens and many other appetizing choices. The prime rib sandwich ($4.25) has satisfied this hungry cyclist on many occasions. The menu also sports a multitude of selections, including fish, chicken, and pasta. The lounge section is decorated with antique toys and bicycles, and offers keno as well. I won $500 once. Open every evening, except Monday, Mister Henry's is an interesting stop for those wanting a complete meal. Prices aren't bad. A T-bone with all the trimmings is a little more than $12.00.

Cafe Carrera is a neat little joint on Fifth and Highway 34. Most peculiarly this restaurant offers food from South of the Border. The diner here should be prepared for large satisfying portions of Mexican cuisine. On one particular occasion, I ordered the "Theresa Special," a mountain of food nearly enough to put me over the edge. If you have any room left for dessert, the Cafe Carrera offers a caboodle of ice cream specialties, including a heaping banana split, creamy malts, and shaky shakes. The decor is simple and the service is friendly. The price nears the are-you-sure-you-charged-me-enough range. Thirty-five of the menu choices are below $3.

Pizza and chicken can be had at the Golden Eagle Keno Lounge after 4 p.m. Diners will have a choice of one topping or combination pizzas. A large, one-topping pizza dents the pocketbook for a mere $10. The Golden Eagle also offers "specially seasoned, hand-breaded chicken" fried to perfection. The four-piece chicken dinner, with choice of two sides, is only $7. The lounge and restaurant occupy one large room, the jukebox is always on, and you'll find the longest bar in a ten-mile radius at 455 South 4th in Eagle.

The most recent addition to the Eagle culinary tour is Grandma's House. Located at 541 So. Fourth, Grandma's is the only place in town to find that all-important meal we call breakfast. Eggs, bacon, and pastries dominate the menu. The "Farmers Breakfast" includes two eggs, four strips of bacon, toast or pancakes, and hash browns. Grandma's also has the only 47 cent cup of coffee I've ever seen. Open from

5:30 a.m. to 5:30 p.m. Monday through Saturday, Grandma's is staffed by none other than a real grandma. Her name is Joan Hesterman and she has sixteen grandchildren. This establishment also serves as her sewing shop, and, according to Grandma Joan, she can "sew anything." The decor is pink, the service is just like grandma's house, and prices are in the "very reasonable" range. The "Big Breakfast" of two eggs, two bacon strips, toast, and hash browns is only $3.

The pretty town of Elmwood completes the MoPac tour. Just recently, however, Elmwood lost its only restaurant. We're hoping another adventurous soul will take up the challenge and re-open the JD Cafe. Hungry bicyclists and townspeople deserve a new watering hole.

As you can see, exploration of the MoPac Trail and its adjoining towns can lead to some unique dining experiences. Each of these towns is just a short bike ride away and all locations are accessible by car. So take a minor risk, seek out these special places, and add your support. The MoPac Trail is a trail for all people; it offers these surprises and many more, so get out and enjoy the trail, as well as some fine dining.

Richard Conradt operates the Walton Trail Company.

Eating Texas: Husker Fans Go South

With the addition of four Texas schools, the Big Eight Conference has become the Big Twelve. The Huskers will feast on Longhorns, Bears, Aggies, and Red Raiders in addition to the usual Wildcat-Buffalo fare. Husker fans might as well eat, too. There are plenty of extraordinary eateries in these four cities of the Lone Star state.

Lubbock - Home of the Texas Tech Red Raiders

Stubb's Bar B Que: Texas-style barbecue and blues.

Fifty-Yard Line: A grubbery popular with media, coaches, and fans. The steaks are named by position. "Tackle" is a T-bone.

Depot Restaurant: Fancier than *Stubb's* or the *Fifty-Yard Line,* known for steaks and prime rib.

Depot Beer Garden: Celebrate the victory under a Texas moon. Not such a good place during a west Texas dust storm.

One Guy from Italy: Located across the street from the campus. Touted as the most authentic Italian in Lubbock; that's like the most authentic Nebraska food in Venice. Think the owner is Italian? His name—believe it or not—Giglomo Mazzameuto.

Waco - Home of the Baylor Bears

Tanglewood Farms: Located across from the campus, voted Waco's best restaurant. Great Texas biscuits, catfish, steaks and chicken-fried steaks.

George's: Heaven for a football fan. When you're not talking football, have a stuffed crab.

Austin - Home of the University of Texas Longhorns

Many brewpubs and great Tex-Mex: Top pubs are *Waterloo Brewing,* the *Bitter End,* and the *Copper Tank.*

Joe's Bakery and Coffee Shop: Classic Tex-Mex. The salsa is just a few thermal units from combustible. Try it, Husker fans; the sensation in your mouth will return eventually. Great fiery chili and huevos rancheros served with chunky red salsa, fried potatoes, bacon, and refried beans.

The Oasis Cantina Del Lago: Tex-Mex with a view. Self-proclaimed Sunset Capital of Texas, the Oasis has a view that'll knock your socks off. It's perched hundreds of feet above Lake Travis outside Austin. Sit on the patio under umbrellas sipping margaritas and munching nachos while you watch the sun go down. Don't go there before the game, you may find it hard to leave.

College Station - Home of the Aggies of Texas A&M

Tom's Bar-B-Que & Steak House: Barbecue served on butcher paper with bread, pickles, onions, and cheddar cheese. The Aggies haven't yet discovered plates (an Aggie joke). The Aggie Special is sausage and smoked meats with the above.

J. D. Wells Rock and Roll Saloon: Music from the sixties through nineties served with the coldest Lone Star Beer in Texas.

My Favorite Place in Nebraska

Andrew Schultz

In my mind, I'm on the north bank of the Platte River, somewhere between Schuyler and Fremont. The cold spring runoff is cooling my heels and as I look south, the budding cottonwoods stand like monuments against the bright clear sky. If everyone has a holy place, mine is here, for the Platte runs through my soul as surely as it runs through this land.

Friends and relatives are buried here, not physically but in my memories and these are more real than grass and stone.

Looking south across the river a sea of grasses stretches miles to the far bluffs. I see and remember that one perfect day when I was ten and helped with the baling. My uncles, all gone now, are here now and at noon, my aunts, Stazie and Josie, bring lunch across the golden field. The only other colors are the electric blue sky and these two aunts walking to us with baskets and dressed in those bright cotton Czech dresses, aprons and babushkas. They look like daubs of paint on a blue and gold canvas.

When I look to my right, I see the island where my father kept his cattle during the summer and I remember getting up with him in the middle of the night to check on them. It is cold, even in July, and the canopy of stars as we get in the truck is so vast that I need to sit right next to him even though I am eight. A wire stretches from the bank of the river to the island and as my father pulls us across the river in the old flat-bottomed boat, the river whispers secrets just beyond knowing.

To my left I see the set lines, and I see my Uncle Anton, a boy even at eighty, bringing in that line full of huge catfish. When I ask him about fighting in the Spanish-American

War, he shakes my hand and says, "I shook hands with Teddy Roosevelt. Pass it on." And I do so to this day.

Further down from the set lines are the duck blinds. I'm four and splashing the river with a stick. Dad is here, Uncle George, a couple of the Kreoger boys and Dukie, Dad's Labrador retriever is dancing to get into the water. He doesn't like me because I always try to ride him. Suddenly the water is over my head and I burst up like a surprised bubble and there is Dukie, grinning. Vengeance is sweet, he is saying.

It's here I returned when I served overseas, when I lived on the coasts, when the dead loneliness of life among strangers was hard and seemed real. It's here I'll come when I die. Norman Maclean wrote, "Eventually, all things merge into one, and a river runs through it." Well, this is my land, my place and this river runs through it.

This essay won the 1996 "My Favorite Place in Nebraska" essay contest sponsored by Nebraska Public Radio. It is printed with permission of the author.

Cats in the Catsup

Southwest of Lincoln, a small-town steakhouse thrived for years. It was famous for huge steaks—the kind that were too big for the plate. After the death of the original owner, the place changed hands several times. The last owner was a lover of cats, any cat, all cats. He fed lots of them, and word spread all over town. Soon lots of cats became lots and lots of cats.

Finally, the love of cats led to cat-astrophe. Lured by sirloin and T-bone, the cats became bold and adventuresome. They hung around the back door; they lounged by the front door; they climbed on the roof; and finally, one invaded the crawl space above the dining room. Cat melodies mingled with the jukebox tunes of Patsy Cline, Johnny Cash, and Waylon Jennings. The steakhouse turned into a cathouse, a cat coup d'etat.

One night during the heart of the take-over, a cat joined us for supper. The creak of an unoiled hinge drew our attention upward. Next came the yeowl of a startled cat. We looked up and across the dining room in time to see a calico cat drop through a loose ceiling panel. The cat plunged into a heap of catsup-covered onion rings.

It's difficult to piece together succeeding events. Some patrons dove for the floor. Others stumbled out of their chairs. We caught glimpses of flying fur and flailing arms. The frenzied cat jumped from the plate to the lap of a burly patron, planting its claws in a T-shirt that strained to cover an enormous belly. The victim attempted to separate himself from the cat. The cat anchored itself more firmly into the T-shirt and belly.

Afraid to touch the attack cat, the large man raised his arms toward heaven. And as he did, he began to warble and shake like a draft horse trying to rid himself of a swarm of horseflies. He shook up and down, then side to side. He continued to warble and shake, then tried an inventive jump-step. But the dance was futile. He could not rid himself of the cat who, in turn, chimed in with the chorus.

At that point the owner, who worked in the kitchen, rushed into the room in his blood-spattered apron. Seeing the owner, the cat-crazed patron began to curse. He cursed, not with cursory curses, but with long, impromptu, creative, and comprehensive curses. The curses embraced the whole of the owner's career, his anatomy, his ancestry, and his aspirations. The curses covered the past and wandered into the distant future. They were fine, substantial curses.

The owner watched, listened, and absorbed the invective. And when the curser stopped, his diatribe spent, he stood quiet and quivering. The owner approached, calmly and lovingly pulling the cat free, leaving four peaks on the white shirt, memorial points of departure.

The owner stroked the cat and sincerely expressed his grief and shock to hear the man give way to temper so. He apologized, and told the man his onion rings were on the house. But this concession did not suffice. The man left under most unpleasant circumstances. A few months later, the formerly famous steakhouse closed.

Cafe Index

Afghani-Kabob 190
Ahmad's 190
Alley Rose 95
Ambrosia Gardens 77
Andy's on First 12
Angie's 199
Anna's 42
Aquarium 173
Argo Hotel 9
Aunt Ruth's 102
Bakery Cafe 72
Barrymore's 143, 206
Big Idea 103
Billy's 144
Bitter End 217
Black Crow 39
Black Dog Diner 94
Blue Heron 145
Blue River Inn 207
Bob's Bar 18
Bogner's 10
Bohemian Cafe 191
Bowring Ranch 73
Brad's Supper Club 86
Brick Wall 115
Bridge Club 76
Bush's Gaslight 128
Butch's Bar 112
Butsy Le Doux's 191
Cafe Carrera 214
Cafe de Paris 173
Cafe on Main 4
Camp Rulo 52
Caniglia's 199
Carey Cottage 13
Carol's Cafe 130
Cassel's 117
Catering Catering 4
Cattleman's (Seneca) 76
Cattlemen's (Lakeside) 132
Cellar 96

Chances R 104
Charlene's 63
Chez Chong 192
City Cafe 20
CJ's 100
Claudia's 174
Coney Island Lunch Room 86
Cookie Company 146
Copper Tank 217
Corner Coffee Shop 22
Cornhusker Hotel 147
Country Inn 120
Country Neighbor 69
Cowpoke Inn 76
Crane River 148
Cuthills Vineyard 23
Cy's 44
Daddy's 18
Danish Baker 66
Dem Bonz 149
Depot Beer Garden 216
Depot Restaurant 216
Diner 74
Doris' Tavern 116
Dotty's Diner 114
Double J-T Cafe and Bar 72
Dowd's 85
Downhome Gourmet 96
Driesbach's 88
Dude's Steak House 134
Dusters 5
Edwardian Lady Tea Room 93
El Alamo 192
El Charitto 136
El Mercadito 151
El Tapatio 89
Empanada House 174
Euni's Palace 111
Fifty Yard Line 216
Flame 133
Flatiron 176

Food Gallery 192
Four Suns 152
Fourth Street Cafe 89
Frankie and Phyl's 196
Fremont Dinner Train 14
French Cafe (Kearney) 97
French Cafe (Omaha) 177
Garden Cafe (Lincoln) 153
Garden Cafe (Omaha) 178
George's 216
Giggling Gourmet 128
Gin's Tavern 75
Glur's Tavern 6
Golden Eagle 214
Golden Nugget 61
Gorat's 199
Grandma Carol's 24
Grandma's House 214
Granny's 39
Greek Islands 193
Green Gables 26
Green Gateau 153
Griffey's 46
Grottos 154
H and I Cafe 193
Habatat 97
Hallie's 49
Harriett's 67
Haskell House 32
Hilltop Inn 118
Hombre Steak House 20
Homemade Heaven Sandwich
    Shop 118
Hungry Horse Saloon 70
Hungry's 11
Husker Bar 28
Hyannis Hotel 70
Imperial Palace (Lincoln) 155
Imperial Palace (Omaha) 194
Imperial Steakhouse 19
Indian Oven 194
Inn Harm's Way 156
Irv's 15

JD Cafe 215
J.D. Wells Saloon 217
J and J City Cafe 100
JaBrisco 156
Jaipur 196
Jan's Strang Tavern 101
Jeanne's 32
Jim's Rib Haven 189
Joe's Bakery & Coffee Shop .. 217
Johnny's Cafe 200
Jordan's 78
K's 157
Keller's II 50
Kiewit Lodge 39
Kolač Cafe 25
Korner Kafe (Byron) 85
Kup 'n Kettle 46
La Mejicana (Hastings) 94
La Mexicana (Grand Island) .. 90
La Strada 72 179
Lazlo's 158
Lebsack's 206
Leonarda's 196
Leprechaun 114
Lied Conference Center 47
Little Deuce Coupe 109
Little Mexico 100
Lo Sole Mio 197
Lobby Restaurant 63
Long Branch 17
M's Pub 180
Magic Wok 43
Mahoney Park 37
Mamasita's 41
Marilyn's Tea Room 3
Market Basket 181
Maxine's 182
Merle's 45
Mi Ranchita 131
Mill 159
Miller & Paine 206
Mister C's 182
Mister Henry's 213

Misty's 160
Molan Bakery 161
Muffin Shoppe 8
My Victorian Heart 129
Naper Cafe 74
Nebraska Inn 71
Nettie's 183
Nick's Main Street Cafe 15
Nila's 69
Nonna's Palazzo 91
Oasis Cantina Del Lago 217
Office Bar and Grill 16
OK Market 31
Old Cafe 54
Old Mill Barbecue 189
Old Vienna Cafe 184
Olde Main Street Inn 127
Ole's Big Game Bar 113
Omaha Prime 200
One Guy From Italy 216
Oregon Trail Wagon Train .. 125
Our Place 59
Oven 161
Papa John's 162
PD Quick Shop 51
Peppercorn 52
Peppermill 78
Picket Fence 8
Piezano's 162
PJ's 109
Plantation 93
Plum Thicket Tea Room 93
PO Pears 163
Pool Hall 111
Porky's 51
Range Cafe 60
Raphael's 197
Renaissance 147
Riley's 33
Rock N Roll Runza 164
Rocket Inn 113
Roost 133
Rosita's 137

Ross' 200
Sale Barn Cafe 46
Salty Dog 53
Sandhills Golf Course xxiii
Sanna's 135
Scribner Hotel Restaurant 28
Simply Desserts 99
Sioux Sundries 129
Skeet's 189
Smet's Cafe 59
Snake Falls Restaurant 79
Sons of Italy 197
Sowders Ranch Store 77
Spanna 184
Sportsman's Steakhouse and
  Lounge 33
Springfield Drug 53
Stable 46
Steak House 165
Stella's 185
Stubb's Bar B Que 216
Sweet Things Bakery 126
Tanglewood Farms 216
Tarbox Hollow Buffalo Ranch 11
Taste of India 166
Ted and Wally's (Lincoln) 166
Ted and Wally's (Omaha) 186
Ted's Tea Room 207
Teresa's 48
Terrace Grille 147
Tex's Cafe 99
Thomas' Tavern 11
Tom's Barbecue & Steak
  House 217
Tony's 64
Top Notch 28
Ulbrick's 48
Uncle Buck's 61
Uptown Eating Establishment
  20
V. Mertz 186
Valentino's 166
Vic's Steakhouse 132

Villa Fiorita 198
Vincenzo's 167
Vivace 187
Walton Trail Co. 213
Watering Hole 207
Waterloo Brewing 217
Wigwam Cafe 29

Wolf's Den 29
Woodshed 138
Yellow Rose 110
YiaYia's 168
Zephyr Cafe 95
Zio's 188

City Index

Ainsworth 59
Alda 85
Anselmo 59
Arnold 210
Ashland 39
Austin 217
Bassett 60
Bayard 125
Beatrice 39
Beemer 3
Bellevue 183, 185
Bennet 41
Blair 4
Boelus 61
Brewster 61
Bridgeport 126
Broken Bow 63
Brownville 212
Byron 85
Cairo 64
Cedar Creek 42
Chadron 127, 211
College Station 217
Columbus 5-8
Cozad 109
Crawford 209
Crete 43
Crofton 9-11
Curtis 110
Dakota City 11
Dannebrog 66-69
David City 11
Dixon 11

Dunning 210
Dwight 44
Eagle 213
Elba 69
Elmwood 215
Elyria 69
Emerald 45
Endicott 207
Ericson 70
Eustis 111
Fairbury 46
Franklin 86
Fremont 12-16, 218
Gering 128-129
Grand Island 86-93, 209
Gross 71
Guide Rock 93
Harrison 129, 211
Harvard 94
Hastings 94
Hayes Center 211
Hemingford 130
Hershey 112
Holdrege 95
Hooper 16
Hyannis 72, 210
Indianola 113
Kearney 95-99
Kimball 131
Lakeside 132
Leshara 17
Lewellen 132
Lexington 114

Lincoln 143-168
Lisco 133
Lubbock 216
Lynch 72
Martinsburg 18
Maywood 211
McCook 211
Melbeta 133
Merriman 73
Milford 46
Minden 100
MoPac Trail 213-215
Mullen .... xxiii, 210
Naper 74
Nebraska City 47-48, 212
Neligh 18-19
Newman Grove 20
Norfolk 20
North Platte ... 115-117, 210, 211
Oakland 22
Ogallala 117-118
Omaha 173-200
Ord 74
Osceola 100
Pawnee City 49
Paxton 119
Peru 212
Pierce 23
Plainview 24
Pleasant Dale 50-51
Prague 25

Republican City 100
Rockville 75
Royal 26
Rulo 52
Schuyler 28, 218
Scottsbluff 136-138
Scribner 28
Seneca 76
Seward 52
Sidney 134-136
Springfield 53
Stanton 29
Steele City 53
Strang 101
Stromsburg 102
Sutton 103
Taylor 76
Tecumseh 54
Thedford 76
Tryon 77, 210
Unadilla 209
Valentine 78-80
Waco 216
Wahoo 29-31
Wakefield 32
Walton 213
Wayne 33
Wellfleet 120
Wynot 33
York 104

Contributor Index

Conradt, Richard 213
Hanna, Robert 1, 37, 57, 83,
          107, 123, 141, 171, 203
Hansen, Ron 82
Homer, Art 170
Kloefkorn, William 122
Kooser, Ted 36

Moul, Francis 209
Raz, Hilda 140
Saiser, Marjorie 106, 202
Scheele, Roy xxvi
Schultz, Andrew 218
Welch, Don 56

Notes